GANN'S MASTER CHARTS UNVEILED

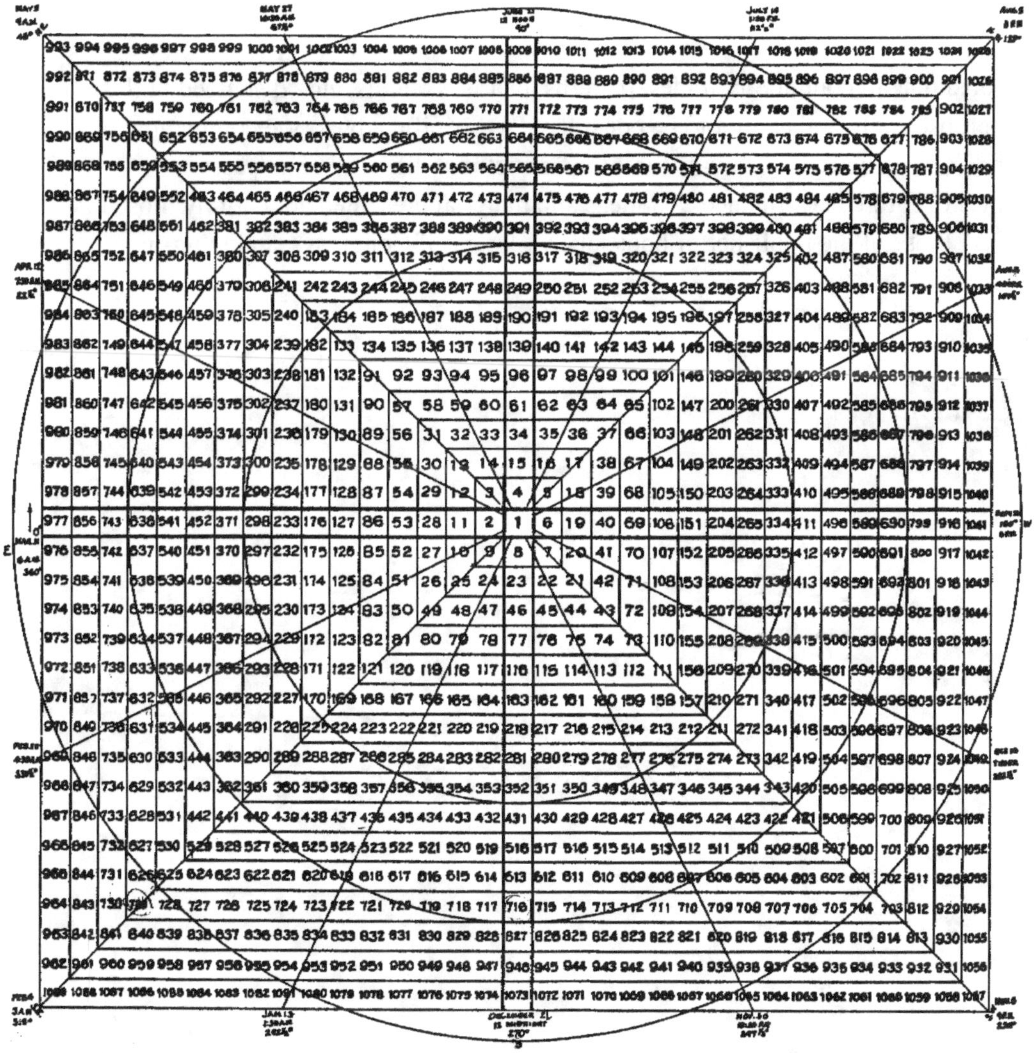

Halliker's, Inc.

Copyright © 2000 Halliker's, Inc.

Published by Halliker's, Inc.

No part of this publication may be reproduced, stored in a retrieval system or transmitted in any form or by any means, electronic, mechanical, photocopying, recording, scanning or otherwise, except as permitted under Sections 107 or 108 of the 1976 United Stated Copyright Act, without either the prior written permission of the Publisher.

The original hand-drawn charts of Gann were reprinted with permission from the Lambert Gann Publishing Co.

This publication is written to provide accurate information in regard to the subject matter covered. It is sold with the understanding that the publisher is not engaged in rendering professional services. If professional advice or other expert assistance is required, the services of a competent professional person should be sought.

CAVEAT: It should be noted that all commodity trades, patterns, charts, systems, etc., discussed in this book are for illustrative purposes only and are not to be considered as specific advisory recommendations. Further note that no method of trading or investing is foolproof or without difficulty, and past performance is no guarantee of future performance. All ideas and material presented are entirely those of the author and do not reflect those of the publisher or bookseller. Library of Congress Cataloging-in-Publication Data:

ISBN-13: 978-1494712181

Printed in the United States of America

Table of Contents

5 Introduction

7 Chapter 1 - Table Charts
7 Square of 20 Fixed - Dow Jones Index
8 Square of 20 Variable - Dow Jones Index
9 Gann's Hand-Drawn NYSE Permanent Chart
10 Gann's Hand-Drawn Square of 360 Chart
11 Master 360 Chart Applied to the Dow Jones Index
12 Gann's Hand-Drawn Sq of 12 Chart
13 Square of 12 Chart - Dec Wheat Weekly
14 Gann's Sq of 12 Hand-Drawn Chart
15 Gann's Hand-Drawn Sq of Low Chart
16 Creating a Table Chart from Scratch

18 Chapter 2 - The Square of Nine
19 The Square of Nine Excel Square
20 Dec Monthly Corn Square of Nine - Price Chart
21 Dec Soybean Meal - Price Chart
25 Dec Corn Monthly Square of Nine - Time Chart
23 Dec Comsilver - Price Chart
24 Xerox Square of Nine - Price Chart
25 Xerox - Square of Nine - Time Chart
26 Gold Square of Nine - Price (downtrend)
27 Gold Monthly Time (Downtrend)
28 Dec Swiss Franc Monthly Square of Nine - Price Chart
29 Changing Cells
31 Enlarging the size of a Chart
32 Changing a Time Square
33 Swiss Franc Monthly Square of Nine - Time Chart

34 Chapter 3 - Square of Four
35 Gann's Example and Use of Square of Four
36 Ganns' Example and Use of the Square of Four - May Coffee
37 Gann's Master Price of Time Chart - Square of Four

38 Chapter 4 - Gann's Ratio Calculator
39 Gann Ratio Calculator - Dec Wheat
40 Gann's Ratio Calculator - A.G. Edwards
41 Chapter 5 - Gann's Hexagon Chart
43 Hexagon Time Chart - November Soybean
44 Hexagon Price Chart - November Soybeans

45 Hexagon Time Chart - November Soybeans

46 Chapter 6 - Circle Charts
49 Gann Hand-Drawn Circle of 72 Chart
50 Gann's Hand-Drawn Circle of 24 Chart
51 Gann's Hand-Drawn Master Time and Price Chart
52 Gann's Hand-Drawn Circle Chart of 36
53 Gann's Hand-Drawn Master 360 Degree Chart
54 The Circle Chart and Astrology
55 Trendlines Represent Planets
56 Proof of Gann's Use of Astrology
57 Japanese Government Bonds Using The Circle Chart
58 Xerox Circle Chart
59 Dec Wheat Circle Chart

60 Chapter 7 - Nine Math Points

62 Chapter 8 - Time/Price Resistance
64 Appendix - Reprints of Square of Nine Articles
65 Predicting Market Trends Using the Square of 9
69 W.D. Gann's The Tunnel Thru the Air
71 In "Sync" With Natural Laws
74 Gann and the Circle
78 Gann's Pyramid and Fourth Factor Volume
82 How to Make the Greatest Profit
86 The Gann Wheel on May 1989 Coffee
87 The Gann Wheel, Octagon Chart, Pythagorean Cube, Square of 9
90 Gann's Secret Pythagorean Cube

99 Bibliography

Introduction

W.D. Gann traded for over 50 years. He wrote several trading books as well as a course on commodities and stocks. It was said that he made over $50 million dollars trading the markets with his mathematical techniques. Because of his success, he became the most famous trader of all time.

Most of Gann's books and courses were written in a veiled language as said by the trading community. What this means is he buried his techniques of trading in his courses. It's there, but the reader has to read and reread his material several times to get anything of trading value out of it. Gann's material is extremely complicated and the trader must have a strong background in mathematics to fully benefit from it. Some expert's think that he did not put in the books and courses what he really traded with, even though the price of the courses was an unbelievable $3,500 at the time he sold them. Converted into today's prices, it would be equilavalent to $50,000. He kept the good trading secrets for himself or for those few who could afford to pay him the asking price of $100,000.

One of the trading methods that Gann kept to himself was the use of Pythagorean Square. He also kept secret the hexagon and the circle charts. He went to the land of the Pyramids to study the Pythagorean Square to find its secrets. It's believed that he found someone over there who explained how it worked and how it could be used in the markets.

We know the Gann used the Pythagorean Square because he was found carrying it with him into the trading pit all the time. This square was hidden in the palm of his hand. How did he use this square? Why did he not discuss the use of this square in his courses? There is only one page covering the Square on Nine in all of his books and courses. Was this square his most valuable tool? These and all the other squares Gann used will be discussed in detail in this book with many illustrations and examples to prove how they work. It almost seems that Gann kept the secret of how to use these charts to himself for two reasons: these charts tell the real mysteries behind the market; and if other traders knew how to use these master charts, it might have hurt his trading.

Virtually every big Gann trader of today that we have questioned has said that they use the Square of Nine in their trading in some way. We have questioned many of these traders and have done much research to help you use these valuable master charts of Gann. The master charts we looked at are the Table Charts, the Square of Nine, the Square of Four, the Hexagon Chart and the Circle Charts and others. We produced this book with charts and illustrations on how to use them to help you trade better and smarter in the markets.

Also included in this book are many of the archived articles previously written in the Gann and Elliott Wave and Traders World magazine on the Square of Nine. These articles are included so you can get a different viewpoints from experts in the field.

Gann Master Charts Unveiled tells you how to use these charts to trade the markets. These charts can be used to calculate natural support and resistance for both time and price. They can also be used to calculate seasonal and calendar time points for market changes.

To support the charts and illustrations a Microsoft Excel Master Template Calculator was developed for each chart presented in the book.

All of these master charts in this book can be used in two different ways. One way is keeping the natural setup of the chart with 1 at the beginning and 1 increment. In this way you would be using the natural or fixed numbers. We call this the fixed method. The other way they can be used is to change the beginning to the bottom or top of a market swing and changing the increment to fit the market price structure. This is called the variable method.

Both of these methods or a combination of these can be used effectively. You should try both to see which fits the market best that you are trading. In the following pages we will go over many examples of both methods.

It is very important to back test any method used in this book with historical data. This data is available from many vendors. We used CSI and the charts contained within this book are from CSI. For more information go to their website at: www.csidata.com By back testing data with the methods in this book or using any method, you gain confidence in your trading. By doing this you see that the method works over and over again and when you are really trading the markets you will have the confidence to successful pull the trigger at the right time and the right place. It's just like a professional athlete, he trains over and over again and when he is out on the field he doesn't have to think when he plays, it becomes automatic. You too, must train over and over again using these methods with historical data before you are ready to go out on the field to play or trade.

Chapter 1
Table Charts

Gann used table charts to find support and resistance in both time and price. The two ways to use the charts are, of course, the fixed and the variable method. The fixed method starts at 1 and the variable method starts with the high or the low of the starting point of the stock or commodity. Gann said that every place that a stock or a commodity stops at, can be figured out using the Square of 20 which is the NYSE Chart, the Square of 12 or the Circle of 360 degrees or the square or the halfway point of some important number. The following chart is the fixed Square of 20 in our Excel chart. These are the natural numbers. See how they hit on the chart. We will explain the Square of 12 and the Circle of 360 degrees later, as well as many other master charts of Gann.

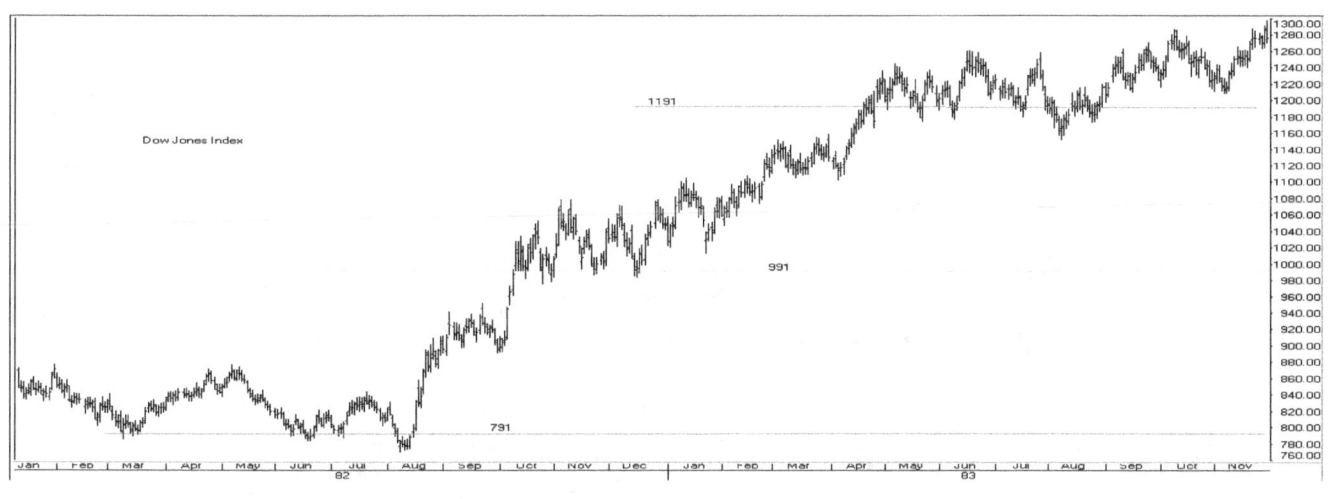

1	2	3	4	5	6	7	8	9	10	11	12	13	14	15	16	17	18	19	20
191	391	591	791	991	1191	1391	1591	1791	1991	2191	2391	2591	2791	2991	3191	3391	3591	3791	3991
181	381	581	781	981	1181	1381	1581	1781	1981	2181	2381	2581	2781	2981	3181	3381	3581	3781	3981
171	371	571	771	971	1171	1371	1571	1771	1971	2171	2371	2571	2771	2971	3171	3371	3571	3771	3971
161	361	561	761	961	1161	1361	1561	1761	1961	2161	2361	2561	2761	2961	3161	3361	3561	3761	3961
151	351	551	751	951	1151	1351	1551	1751	1951	2151	2351	2551	2751	2951	3151	3351	3551	3751	3951
141	341	541	741	941	1141	1341	1541	1741	1941	2141	2341	2541	2741	2941	3141	3341	3541	3741	3941
131	331	531	731	931	1131	1331	1531	1731	1931	2131	2331	2531	2731	2931	3131	3331	3531	3731	3931
121	321	521	721	921	1121	1321	1521	1721	1921	2121	2321	2521	2721	2921	3121	3321	3521	3721	3921
111	311	511	711	911	1111	1311	1511	1711	1911	2111	2311	2511	2711	2911	3111	3311	3511	3711	3911
101	301	501	701	901	1101	1301	1501	1701	1901	2101	2301	2501	2701	2901	3101	3301	3501	3701	3901
91	291	491	691	891	1091	1291	1491	1691	1891	2091	2291	2491	2691	2891	3091	3291	3491	3691	3891
81	281	481	681	881	1081	1281	1481	1681	1881	2081	2281	2481	2681	2881	3081	3281	3481	3681	3881
71	271	471	671	871	1071	1271	1471	1671	1871	2071	2271	2471	2671	2871	3071	3271	3471	3671	3871
61	261	461	661	861	1061	1261	1461	1661	1861	2061	2261	2461	2661	2861	3061	3261	3461	3661	3861
51	251	451	651	851	1051	1251	1451	1651	1851	2051	2251	2451	2651	2851	3051	3251	3451	3651	3851
41	241	441	641	841	1041	1241	1441	1641	1841	2041	2241	2441	2641	2841	3041	3241	3441	3641	3841
31	231	431	631	831	1031	1231	1431	1631	1831	2031	2231	2431	2631	2831	3031	3231	3431	3631	3831
21	221	421	621	821	1021	1221	1421	1621	1821	2021	2221	2421	2621	2821	3021	3221	3421	3621	3821
11	211	411	611	811	1011	1211	1411	1611	1811	2011	2211	2411	2611	2811	3011	3211	3411	3611	3811
1	201	401	601	801	1001	1201	1401	1601	1801	2001	2201	2401	2601	2801	3001	3201	3401	3601	3801

Begin	1
Incre	10
Name	DJIA

Square of 20 Variable – Dow Jones Index

The beginning can also be changed to give you a variable square which can be used to find resistance in both time and price. The following DJIA chart starts off at 770. You can see major resistance and support at the top and bottoms indicated by the variable Square of 20 Chart. You will also see support and resistance at the diagonal and horizontal price lines on the Square of 20 Chart.

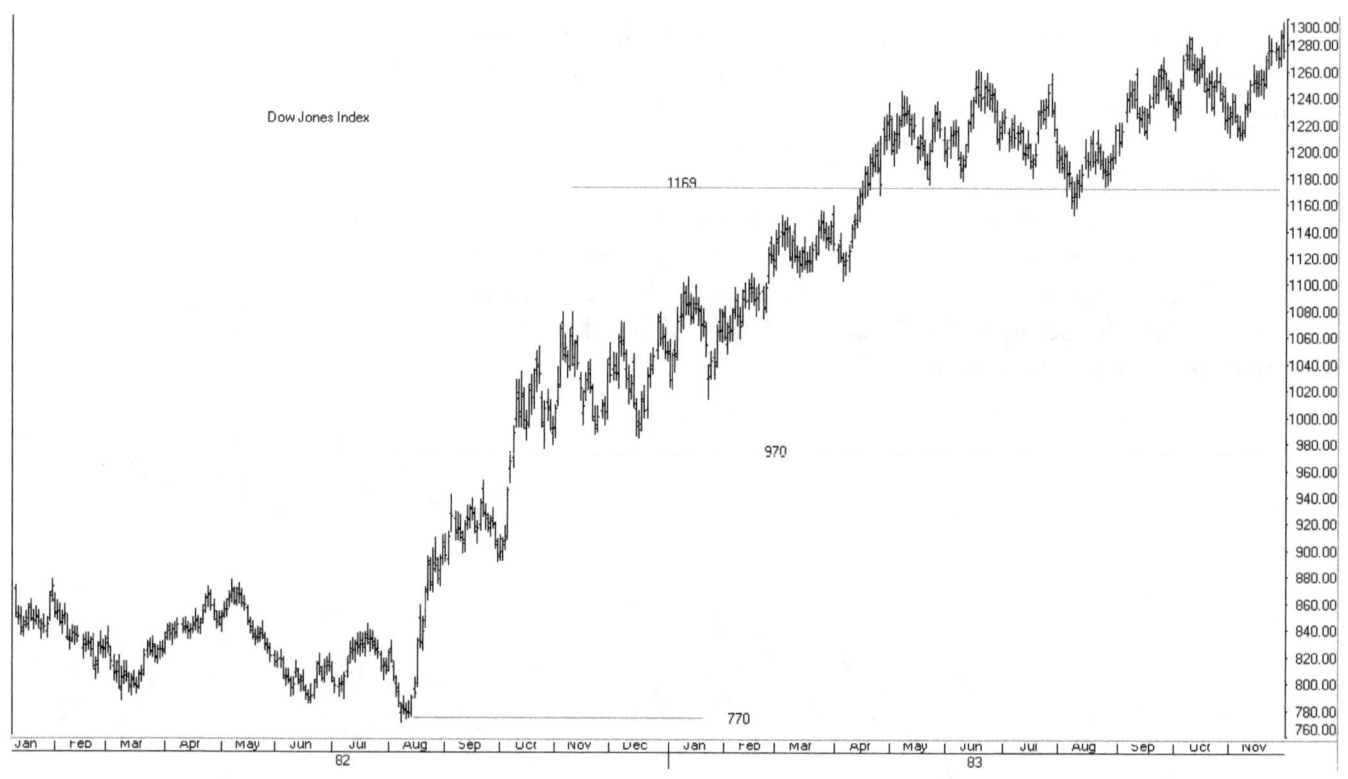

1	2	3	4	5	6	7	8	9	10	11	12	13	14	15	16	17	18	19	20
789	809	829	849	869	889	909	929	949	969	989	1009	1029	1049	1069	1089	1109	1129	1149	1169
788	808	828	848	868	888	908	928	948	968	988	1008	1028	1048	1068	1088	1108	1128	1148	1168
787	807	827	847	867	887	907	927	947	967	987	1007	1027	1047	1067	1087	1107	1127	1147	1167
786	806	826	846	866	886	906	926	946	966	986	1006	1026	1046	1066	1086	1106	1126	1146	1166
785	805	825	845	865	885	905	925	945	965	985	1005	1025	1045	1065	1085	1105	1125	1145	1165
784	804	824	844	864	884	904	924	944	964	984	1004	1024	1044	1064	1084	1104	1124	1144	1164
783	803	823	843	863	883	903	923	943	963	983	1003	1023	1043	1063	1083	1103	1123	1143	1163
782	802	822	842	862	882	902	922	942	962	982	1002	1022	1042	1062	1082	1102	1122	1142	1162
781	801	821	841	861	881	901	921	941	961	981	1001	1021	1041	1061	1081	1101	1121	1141	1161
780	800	820	840	860	880	900	920	940	960	980	1000	1020	1040	1060	1080	1100	1120	1140	1160
779	799	819	839	859	879	899	919	939	959	979	999	1019	1039	1059	1079	1099	1119	1139	1159
778	798	818	838	858	878	898	918	938	958	978	998	1018	1038	1058	1078	1098	1118	1138	1158
777	797	817	837	857	877	897	917	937	957	977	997	1017	1037	1057	1077	1097	1117	1137	1157
776	796	816	836	856	876	896	916	936	956	976	996	1016	1036	1056	1076	1096	1116	1136	1156
775	795	815	835	855	875	895	915	935	955	975	995	1015	1035	1055	1075	1095	1115	1135	1155
774	794	814	834	854	874	894	914	934	954	974	994	1014	1034	1054	1074	1094	1114	1134	1154
773	793	813	833	853	873	893	913	933	953	973	993	1013	1033	1053	1073	1093	1113	1133	1153
772	792	812	832	852	872	892	912	932	952	972	992	1012	1032	1052	1072	1092	1112	1132	1152
771	791	811	831	851	871	891	911	931	951	971	991	1011	1031	1051	1071	1091	1111	1131	1151
770	790	810	830	850	870	890	910	930	950	970	990	1010	1030	1050	1070	1090	1110	1130	1150

Begin	770
Incre	1
Name	DJIA

Gann's Hand-Drawn NYSE Permanent Chart

The below chart is the Sq of 20 Chart (that's 20 squares up and 20 squares over) that Gann actually used. He had to write in all the numbers by hand. It did the job, even though it does not look as neat and clean as our Excel charts.

NYSE PERMANENT CHART

1	2	3	4	5	6	7	8	9	10	11	12	13	14	15	16	17	18	19	20
20	40	60	80	100	120	140	160	180	200	220	240	260	280	300	320	340	360	380	400
19	39	59	79	99	119	139	159	179	199	219	239	259	279	299	319	339	359	379	399
18	38	58	78	98	118	138	158	178	198	218	238	258	278	298	318	338	358	378	398
17	37	57	77	97	117	137	157	177	197	217	237	257	277	297	317	337	357	377	397
16	36	56	76	96	116	136	156	176	196	216	236	256	276	296	316	336	356	376	396
15	35	55	75	95	115	135	155	175	195	215	235	255	275	295	315	335	355	375	395
14	34	54	74	94	114	134	154	174	194	214	234	254	274	294	314	334	354	374	394
13	33	53	73	93	113	133	153	173	193	213	233	253	273	293	313	333	353	373	393
12	32	52	72	92	112	132	152	172	192	212	232	252	272	292	312	332	352	372	392
11	31	51	71	91	111	131	151	171	191	211	231	251	271	291	311	331	351	371	391
10	30	50	70	90	110	130	150	170	190	210	230	250	270	290	310	330	350	370	390
9	29	49	69	89	109	129	149	169	189	209	229	249	269	289	309	329	349	369	389
8	28	48	68	88	108	128	148	168	188	208	228	248	268	288	308	328	348	368	388
7	27	47	67	87	107	127	147	167	187	207	227	247	267	287	307	327	347	367	387
6	26	46	66	86	106	126	146	166	186	206	226	246	266	286	306	326	346	366	386
5	25	45	65	85	105	125	145	165	185	205	225	245	265	285	305	325	345	365	385
4	24	44	64	84	104	124	144	164	184	204	224	244	264	284	304	324	344	364	384
3	23	43	63	83	103	123	143	163	183	203	223	243	263	283	303	323	343	363	383
2	22	42	62	82	102	122	142	162	182	202	222	242	262	282	302	322	342	362	382
1	21	41	61	81	101	121	141	161	181	201	221	241	261	281	301	321	341	361	381

MAY 17, 1792

W.D. GANN

Gann's Hand-Drawn Square of 360 Chart

As we mentioned above, Gann also used the 360-degree chart to forecast important support and resistance points. Here is the one that he constructed. He started it with 15 with increments of 15. He called this his Master 360 Chart. Notice that he put divisions and degrees on the outside of this chart. You can also do that with the Excel charts that are available on your template CD that is furnished with this book.

Master 360 Chart Applied to the Dow Jones Index

This is the Master 360 Chart set to begin at 15 with increments of 15, just like Gann's hand-drawn one. See how the chart prices respects the horizontal division lines of the Master 360 Chart. In the move up prices clearly stop at these important price levels.

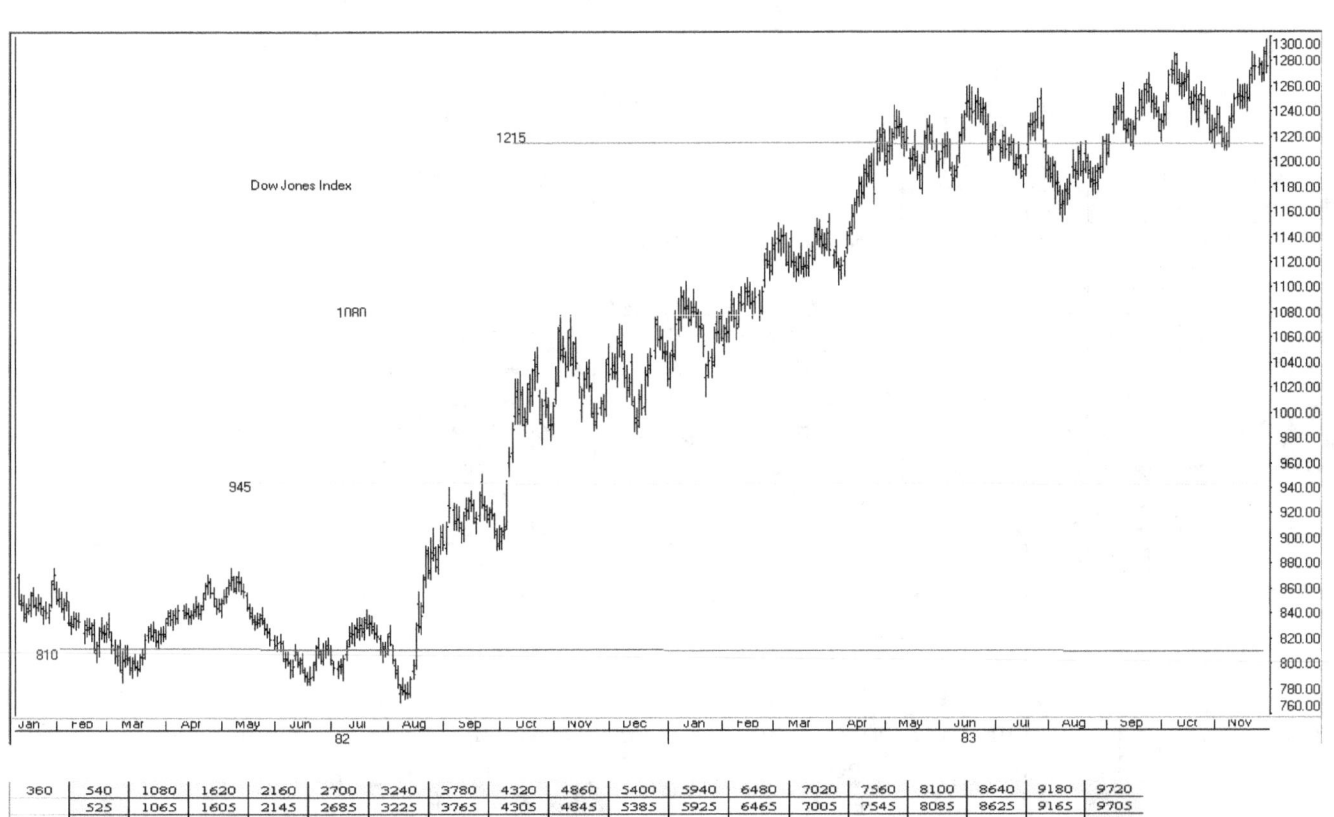

Gann's Hand-Drawn Square of 12 Chart

In the following chart you can see how Gann used the Sq of 12 to calculate time and price from 1 to 30 years. 30 years is ½ the master time factor of 60 years. This chart clearly shows the important time periods to watch for. Study this chart carefully as it is the secret to successful long term trading using historical data.

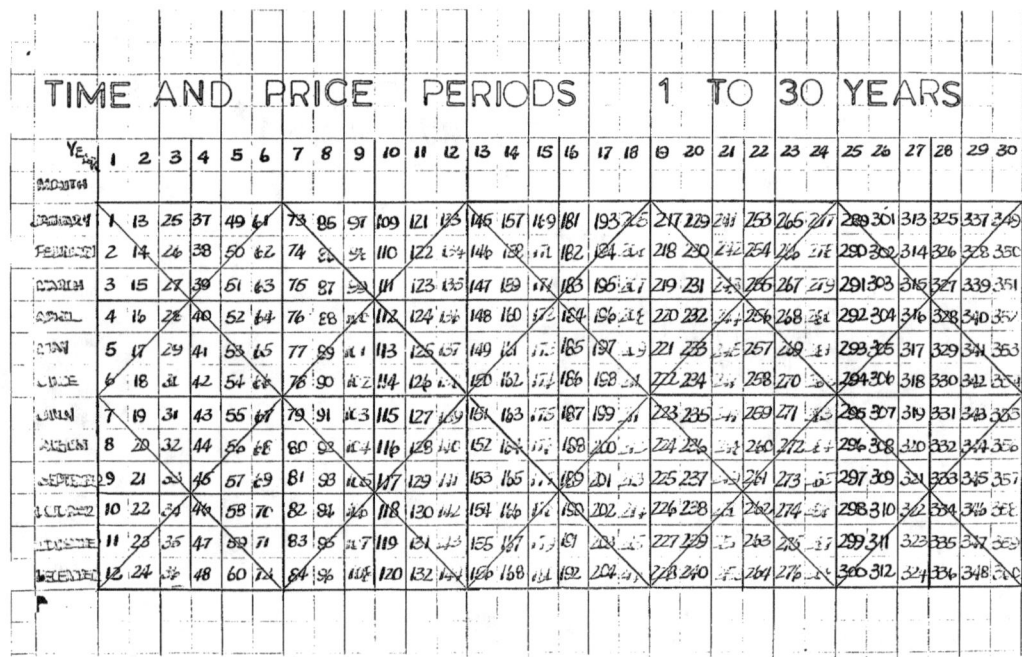

Below is the Sq of 12 Chart in Excel format, which can be easily used in both fixed and variable format. We have changed the format slightly so the beginning number starts out at the bottom to keep it consistent with our other charts. It still serves it's purpose. The bottom and the top as well as the divisions thereof and even the diagonals represent support and resistance levels in both time and price. See how neat and clean this chart is. Remember you can label the outside parameter with the names of months, just as Gann did in his hand-drawn example.

12	24	36	48	60	72	84	96	108	120	132	144	156	168	180	192	204	216	228	240	252	264	276	288
11	23	35	47	59	71	83	95	107	119	131	143	155	167	179	191	203	215	227	239	251	263	275	287
10	22	34	46	58	70	82	94	106	118	130	142	154	166	178	190	202	214	226	238	250	262	274	286
9	21	33	45	57	69	81	93	105	117	129	141	153	165	177	189	201	213	225	237	249	261	273	285
8	20	32	44	56	68	80	92	104	116	128	140	152	164	176	188	200	212	224	236	248	260	272	284
7	19	31	43	55	67	79	91	103	115	127	139	151	163	175	187	199	211	223	235	247	259	271	283
6	18	30	42	54	66	78	90	102	114	126	138	150	162	174	186	198	210	222	234	246	258	270	282
5	17	29	41	53	65	77	89	101	113	125	137	149	161	173	185	197	209	221	233	245	257	269	281
4	16	28	40	52	64	76	88	100	112	124	136	148	160	172	184	196	208	220	232	244	256	268	280
3	15	27	39	51	63	75	87	99	111	123	135	147	159	171	183	195	207	219	231	243	255	267	279
2	14	26	38	50	62	74	86	98	110	122	134	146	158	170	182	194	206	218	230	242	254	266	278
1	13	25	37	49	61	73	85	97	109	121	133	145	157	169	181	193	205	217	229	241	253	265	277

Begin	1
Incre	1
Name	

Square of 12 Chart - Dec Wheat Weekly

This is an example using the Sq of 12 Chart with Dec Wheat Weekly. Notice how the highs and lows of the move often hit either at the top or the bottom of the Sq of 12. Also notice how the divisions of the Square of 12 also show support and resistance. Also, notice how the prices on the chart hit or come close to the diagonals on the Sq of 12. As you can see, the Sq of 12 is a very important master chart to have around.

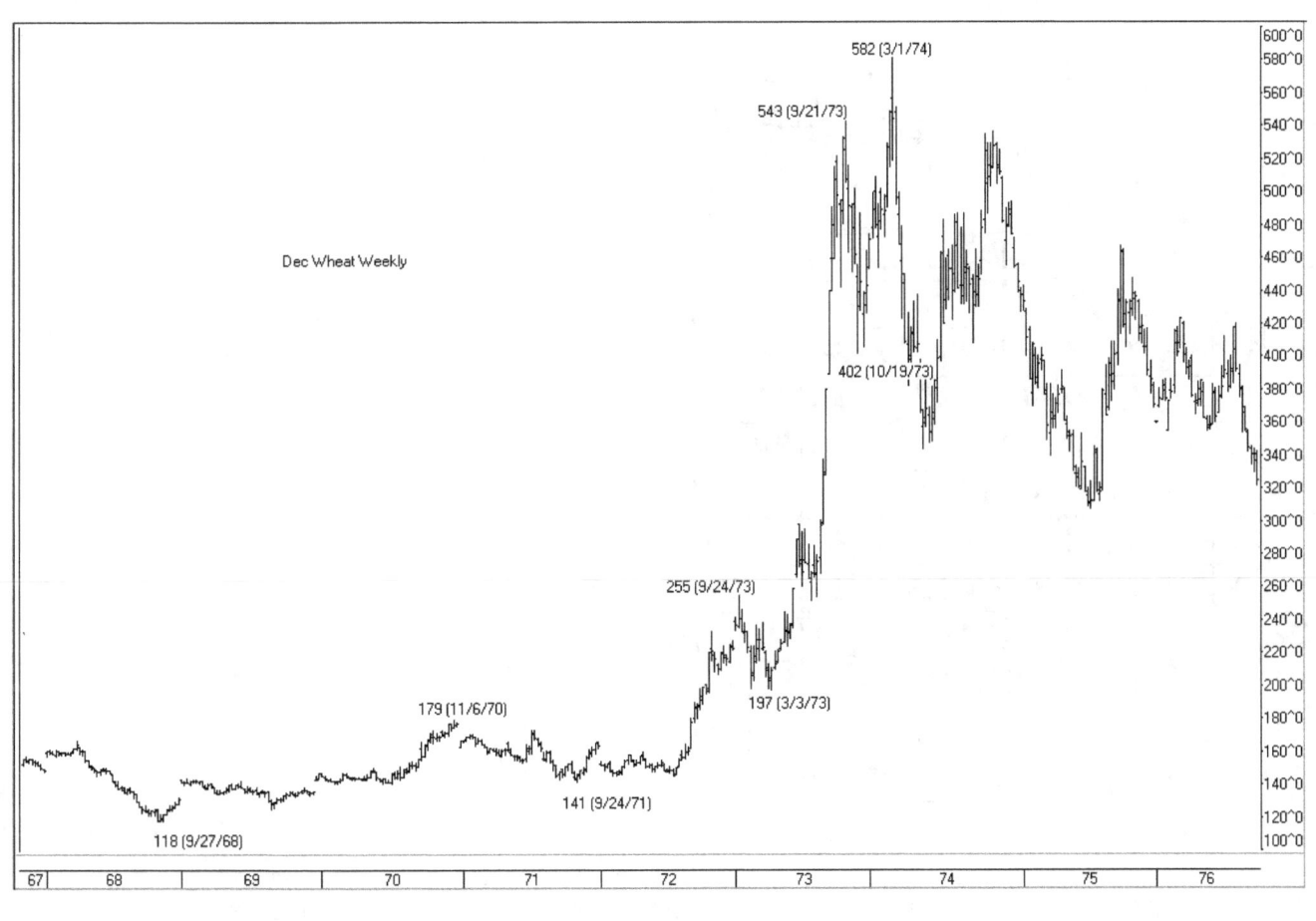

Gann's Square of 12 Hand-Drawn Chart

Here is another example of a Gann Sq of 12 Chart using 31 as the beginning number and an increment of 30. Gann used this as a time chart to tell the important timing points of the year. Study it carefully; it will be beneficial to you. Notice how he has labeled the months of the year on the top of his chart. Remember you can also label the Excel charts just like this example. Our Excel template, which can be used to calculate both fixed and variable time and price points, is at the bottom of this page.

Gann's Hand-Drawn Sq of Low Chart

This is an example of using a low to calculate areas of support and resistance. You can do this with any high or low with the Excel software program. The next page explains this step-by-step procedure. It takes a little more time, but the result is worth the effort. Please put the work into these charts and you will be financially rewarded.

Creating a Table Chart from Scratch
Step 1
Go to the Excel program and create a new worksheet.

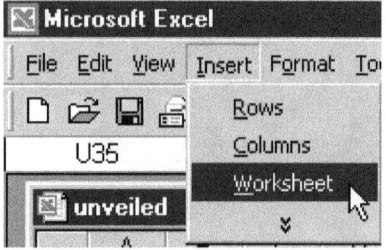

Step 2
Label it on the bottom

Step 3
Setup your Begin, Incre, and Name boxes. Make your first cell start with +b45 plus your incre cell of +b46.

44		
45	Begin	
46	Incre	
47	Name	

Step 4
Start at the bottom with the beginning number. In the Gann example above it was 44. Insert the formula (+a43+b46) in cell a42.

41		
42	45	
43	44	
44		
45	Begin	44
46	Incre	1
47	Name	

Step 5
Now, do the same to cell a41. Insert the formula (b42+B46).

41	46	
42	45	
43	44	
44		
45	Begin	44
46	Incre	1
47	Name	

Step 6
Do this same thing all the way up and start over at the bottom and go up again.

Step 7
Finish the chart with the necessary columns you need.

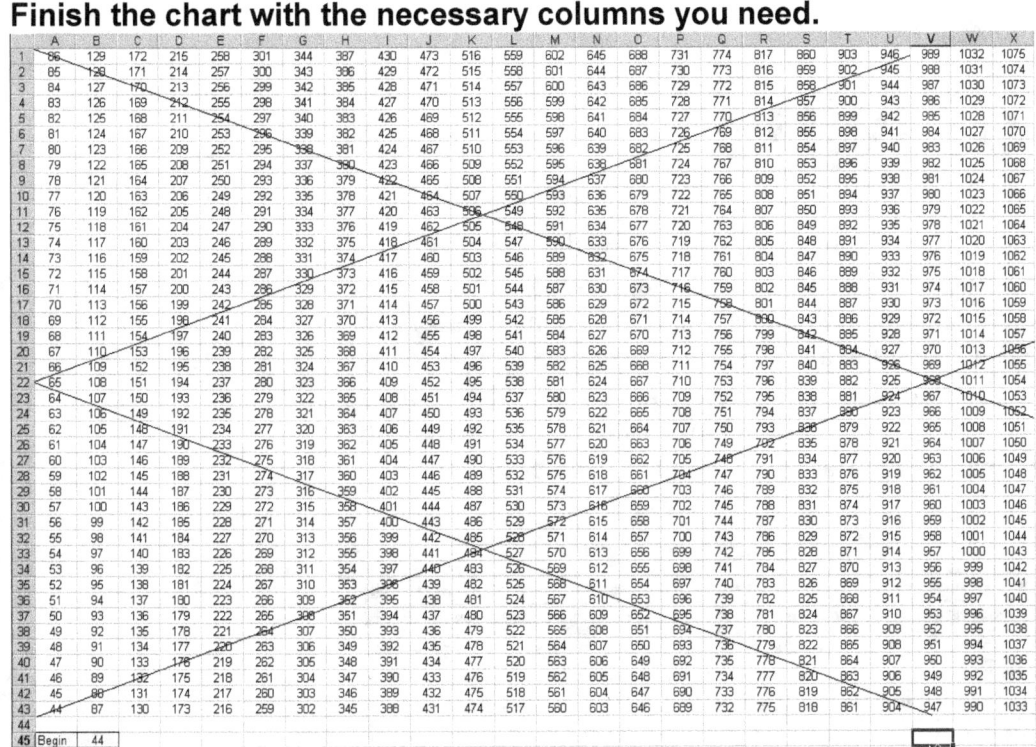

Step 8
You can now draw the trendlines on the chart using the draw trendline function at the bottom of the Excel program.

Step 9
You can now set or change the Begin to any number you want and change the Increment to any number. The entire Excel chart will change at your command.

Begin	44
Incre	1
Name	

Chapter 2
Square of Nine

This is Gann's Square of Nine Chart, which he setup and drew the numbers by hand. He used a compass and rulers to draw the circular and straight lines. The purpose of this square is to give you support and resistance in the markets for both price and time. This square can be used in any time frame. (minute, hourly, daily, weekly, quarterly or yearly). The chart can be set fixed with a starting point of 1 and an increment of 1 or variable using bottoms and tops with various increments. Yearly calendar dates can be put on the parameter as well as degrees of the circle.

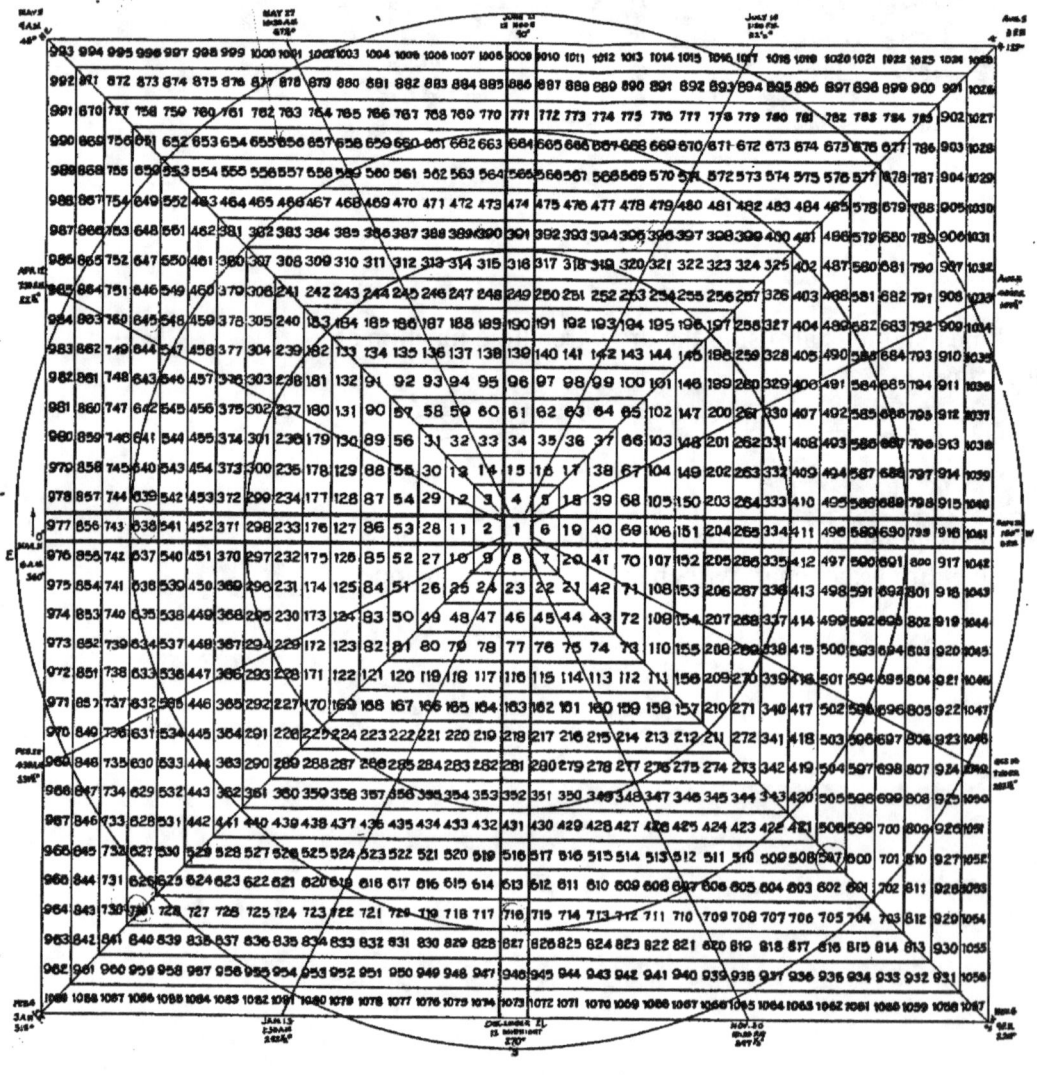

The Square of Nine Excel Square

This is the Square of Nine Chart, which we setup in Excel. It is the same as Gann's hand-drawn chart. It has the advantage giving you the ability to begin it with and number and set the increment to any number you wish, either a positive or a negative increment for both tops and bottoms.

This basic chart starts with the number 1 at the center and expands outwardly adding 1 number per square in a clockwise manner. You can use the chart this way, or in a fixed manner using the natural numbers.

239	240	241	242	243	244	245	246	247	247	247	247	247	247	247	247	247
238	183	184	185	186	187	188	189	190	191	192	193	194	194	194	195	248
237	182	133	134	135	136	137	138	139	140	141	142	143	144	145	196	249
236	181	132	91	92	93	94	95	96	97	98	99	100	101	146	197	250
235	180	131	90	57	58	59	60	61	62	63	64	65	102	147	198	251
234	179	130	89	56	31	32	33	34	35	36	37	66	103	148	199	252
233	178	129	88	55	30	13	14	15	16	17	38	67	104	149	200	253
232	177	128	87	54	29	12	3	4	5	18	39	68	105	150	201	254
231	176	127	86	53	28	11	2	1	6	19	40	69	106	151	202	255
230	175	126	85	52	27	10	9	8	7	20	41	70	107	152	203	256
229	174	125	84	51	26	25	24	23	22	21	42	71	108	153	204	257
228	173	124	83	50	49	48	47	46	45	44	43	72	109	154	205	258
227	172	123	82	81	80	79	78	77	76	75	74	73	110	155	206	259
226	171	122	121	120	119	118	117	116	115	114	113	112	111	156	207	260
225	170	169	168	167	166	165	164	163	162	161	160	159	158	157	208	261
224	223	222	221	220	219	218	217	216	215	214	213	212	211	210	209	262
279	278	277	276	275	274	273	272	271	270	269	268	267	266	265	264	263

Begin	1
Incre	1
Name	

You need to input two variables to create a variable chart. The two points you need to set are the beginning point of the market and the increment of the increase or decrease per square.

In an uptrend you put the low at the center of the square. You need then to decide on the increment of the increase per square. You normally need to use .001, .01. 1, 10, 100. You can also split that and go to .0005, .005, .05, .5, 5, 50 and so on.

In a downtrend the high of a reaction should be put in the center. You would again decide on the increment of the decrease per square. Use again the same numbers as above, but with a minus sign in front. Use the -.001, -.01, -.1, -1, -10, -100 or the -.0005, -.005, -.05, -.5, -5, -50 etc.

This is where you put the beginning and increment numbers. You can also put in the name of the market you are analyzing, if you wish.

Begin	1
Incre	1
Name	

Dec Monthly Corn Square of Nine – Price Chart

In the example below, we show December Corn. In the Square of Nine Price Chart we set the beginning to the low of 101 in 1968. Set the increment to 1. Notice the lows and highs all the way up in the trend were exactly on key points on the Square of Nine Chart.

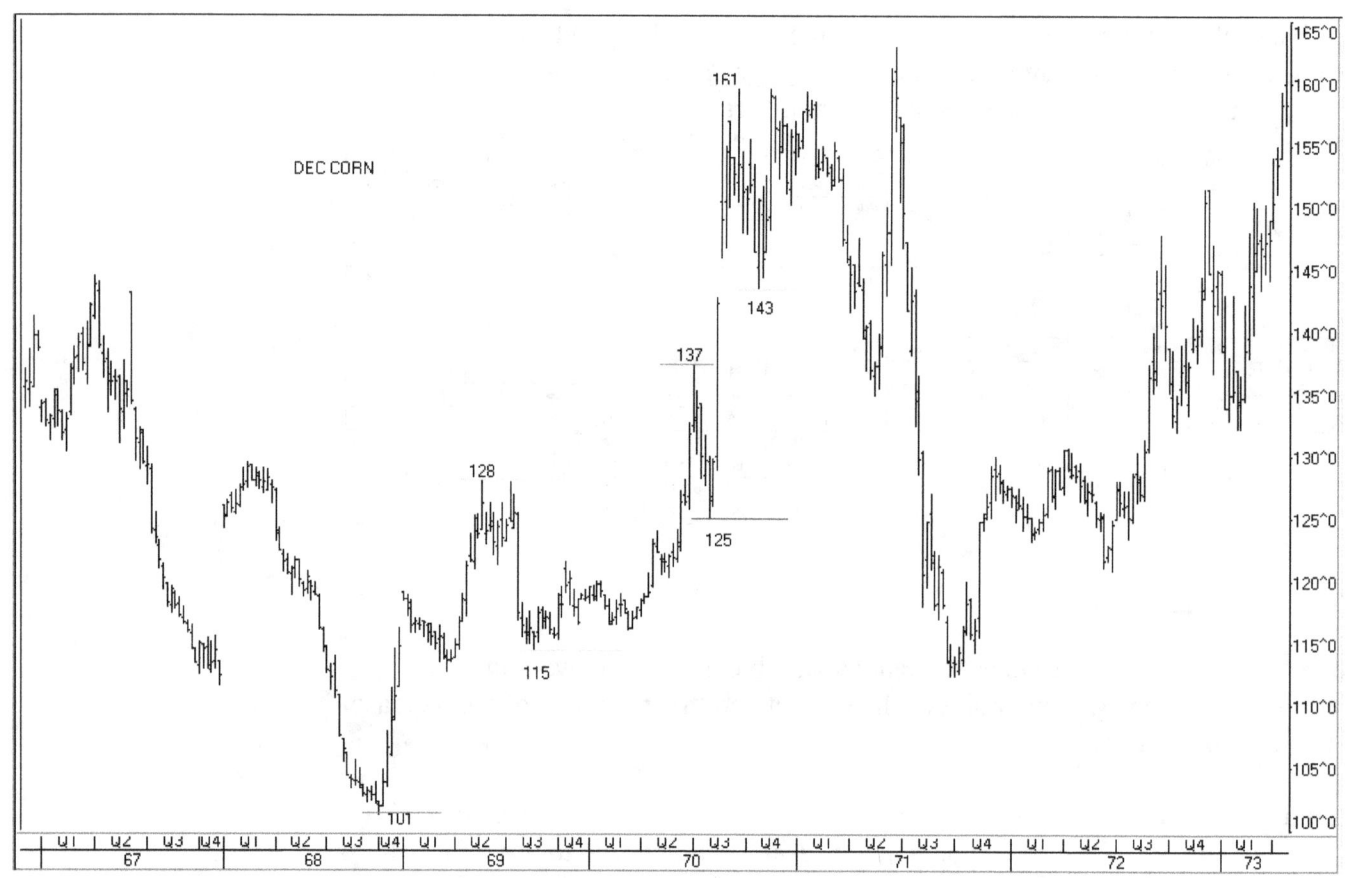

Dec Soybean Meal - Price Chart

In this Soybean Meal example we set the beginning at 43 and the increment at 1. Look at how the highs and lows on the price chart hit on the support and resistance lines on the Square of Nine Chart.. It's quite amazing.

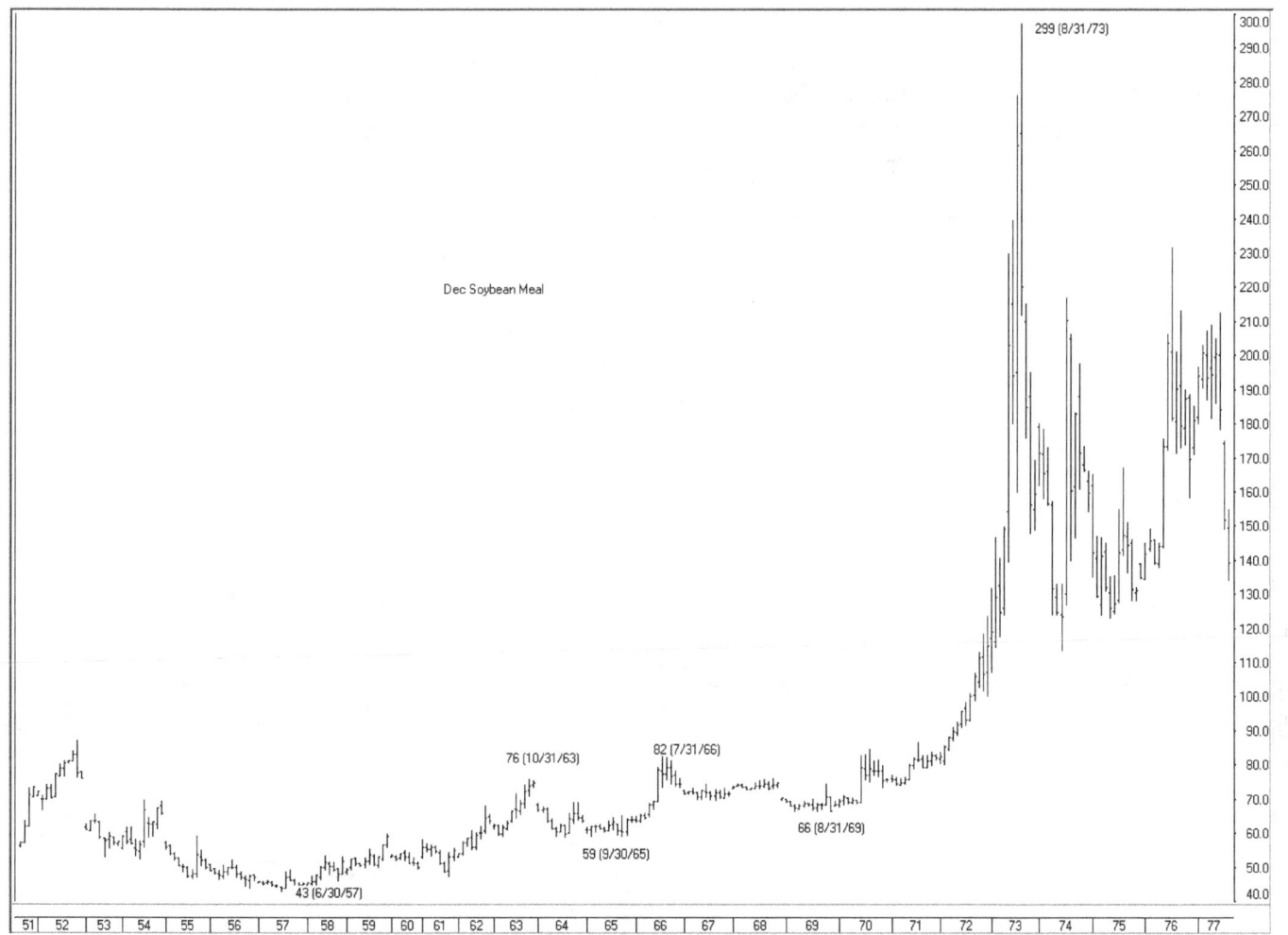

Dec Corn Monthly Square of Nine – Time Chart

You can also change the Square of Nine to a date chart. In this example of December Corn monthly, we set the beginning date at 10/4/68 on the Square of Nine Chart. Set the increment to 1. Notice the large number of hits on the Square of Nine Chart close to the resistance lines. Remember that when you advance in time to a resistance point on this chart, the time date in the Square of Nine represents a barrier. Sometimes the market is not strong enough to get through this barrier. It may even fail several days before. Sometimes if the strength of the market is very strong it has the power to go through the resistance lines, but then it will usually fall back under the resistance line again.

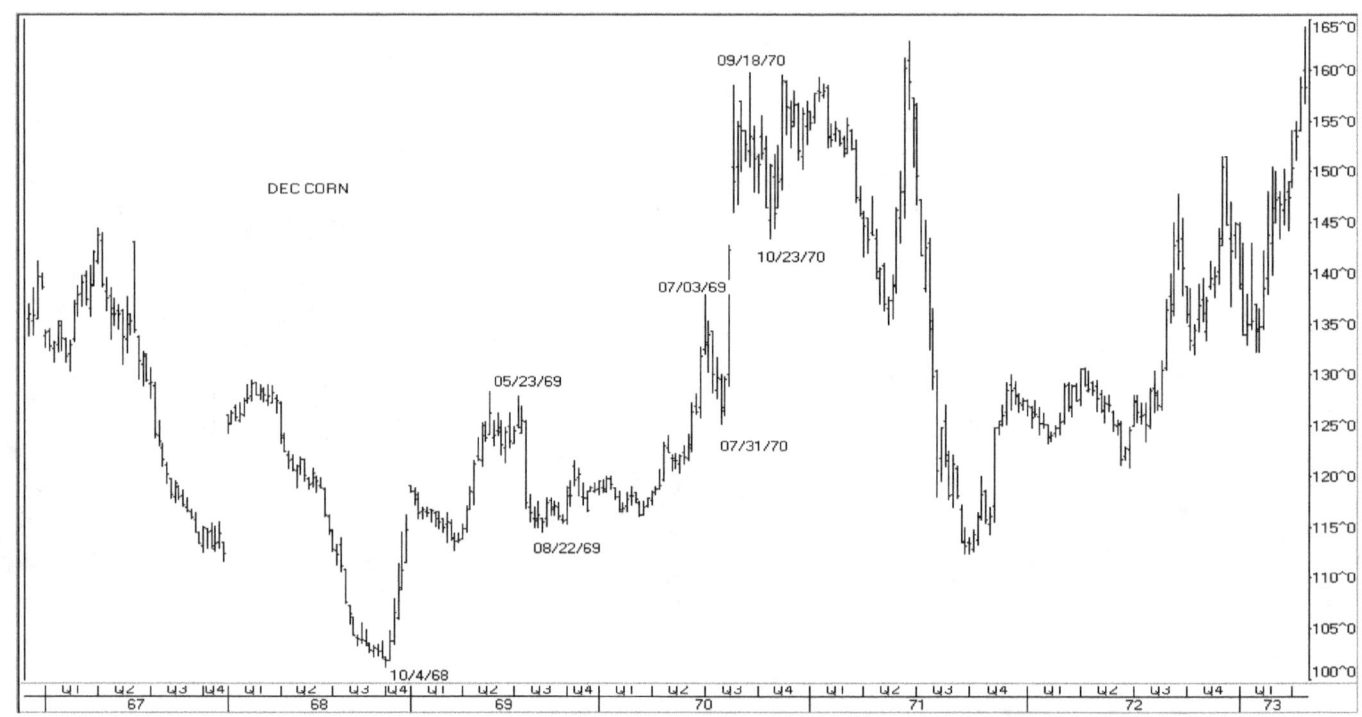

Dec Comsilver – Price Chart

Notice in this example of December Comsilver using the Square of Nine price chart, the big run-up in prices and how it hit the resistance and support lines. It's clear that you can successfully use these important prices to trade off of. Combine these prices with other techniques of trading to increase the effectiveness of the signals.

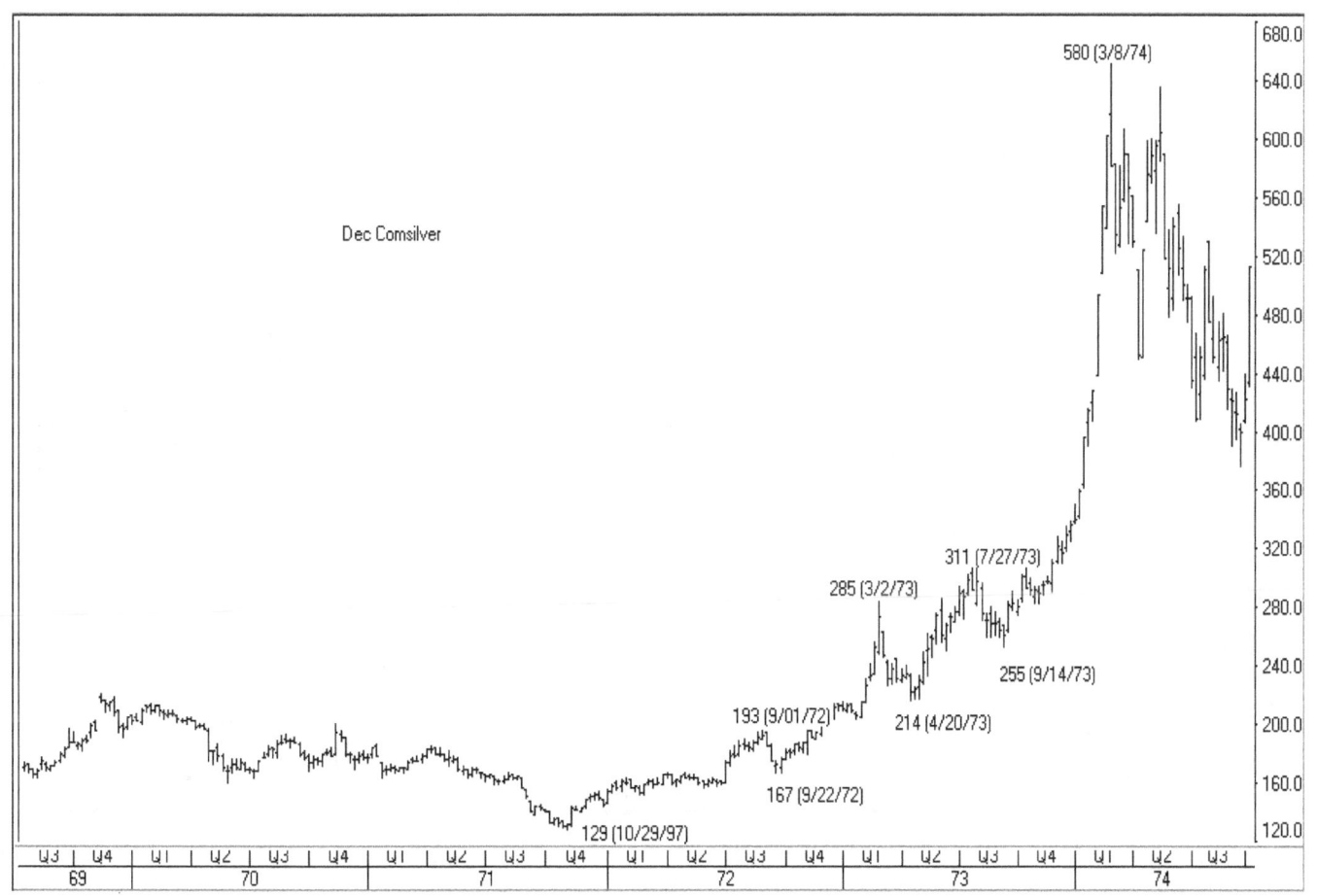

Xerox Square of Nine – Price Chart

In this Xerox chart we set the beginning point at 20, which was the low and the increment to 1. You can see the market stops almost exactly at the resistance lines on the Square of Nine all the way up. This is just one more example of the effectiveness of the Square of Nine. You should continue to practice with historical data and check out the importance of the magical Square of Nine.

203	204	205	206	207	208	209	210	211	212	213	214
152	153	154	155	156	157	158	159	160	161	162	163
151	110	111	112	113	114	115	116	117	118	119	120
150	109	76	77	78	79	80	81	82	83	84	121
149	108	75	50	51	52	53	54	55	56	85	122
148	107	74	49	32	33	34	35	36	57	86	123
147	106	73	48	31	22	23	24	37	58	87	124
146	105	72	47	30	21	20	25	38	59	88	125
145	104	71	46	29	28	27	26	39	60	89	126
144	103	70	45	44	43	42	41	40	61	90	127
143	102	69	68	67	66	65	64	63	62	91	128
142	101	100	99	98	97	96	95	94	93	92	129
141	140	139	138	137	136	135	134	133	132	131	130

Xerox – Square of Nine – Time Chart

In this Square of Nine Chart we changed it to a time chart and set the beginning date at 11/6/96 and the increment to 1. Notice how many of the dates stopped exactly on or just before the resistance lines. Use these resistance and support dates to trade more effectively. Gann always said that time was the most important factor. That means that you check out time before anything else. Price is secondary. When time stops going up, the market will eventually decline.

2/4/97	2/5/97	2/6/97	2/7/97	2/8/97	2/9/97	2/10/97	2/11/97	2/12/97	2/13/97	2/14/97	3/31/97	5/23/97	7/23/97
2/3/97	1/1/97	1/2/97	1/3/97	1/4/97	1/5/97	1/6/97	1/7/97	1/8/97	1/9/97	2/15/97	4/1/97	5/24/97	7/24/97
2/2/97	12/31/96	12/6/96	12/7/96	12/8/96	12/9/96	12/10/96	12/11/96	12/12/96	1/10/97	2/16/97	4/2/97	5/25/97	7/25/97
2/1/97	12/30/96	12/5/96	11/18/96	11/19/96	11/20/96	11/21/96	11/22/96	12/13/96	1/11/97	2/17/97	4/3/97	5/26/97	7/26/97
1/31/97	12/29/96	12/4/96	11/17/96	11/8/96	11/9/96	11/10/96	11/23/96	12/14/96	1/12/97	2/18/97	4/4/97	5/27/97	7/27/97
1/30/97	12/28/96	12/3/96	11/16/96	11/7/96	11/6/96	11/11/96	11/24/96	12/15/96	1/13/97	2/19/97	4/5/97	5/28/97	7/28/97
1/29/97	12/27/96	12/2/96	11/15/96	11/14/96	11/13/96	11/12/96	11/25/96	12/16/96	1/14/97	2/20/97	4/6/97	5/29/97	7/29/97
1/28/97	12/26/96	12/1/96	11/30/96	11/29/96	11/28/96	11/27/96	11/26/96	12/17/96	1/15/97	2/21/97	4/7/97	5/30/97	7/30/97
1/27/97	12/25/96	12/24/96	12/23/96	12/22/96	12/21/96	12/20/96	12/19/96	12/18/96	1/16/97	2/22/97	4/8/97	5/31/97	7/31/97
1/26/97	1/25/97	1/24/97	1/23/97	1/22/97	1/21/97	1/20/97	1/19/97	1/18/97	1/17/97	2/23/97	4/9/97	6/1/97	8/1/97
3/6/97	3/5/97	3/4/97	3/3/97	3/2/97	3/1/97	2/28/97	2/27/97	2/26/97	2/25/97	2/24/97	4/10/97	6/2/97	8/2/97
4/22/97	4/21/97	4/20/97	4/19/97	4/18/97	4/17/97	4/16/97	4/15/97	4/14/97	4/13/97	4/12/97	4/11/97	6/3/97	8/3/97
6/16/97	6/15/97	6/14/97	6/13/97	6/12/97	6/11/97	6/10/97	6/9/97	6/8/97	6/7/97	6/6/97	6/5/97	6/4/97	8/4/97
8/18/97	8/17/97	8/16/97	8/15/97	8/14/97	8/13/97	8/12/97	8/11/97	8/10/97	8/9/97	8/8/97	8/7/97	8/6/97	8/5/97
10/28/97	10/27/97	10/26/97	10/25/97	10/24/97	10/23/97	10/22/97	10/21/97	10/20/97	10/19/97	10/18/97	10/17/97	10/16/97	10/15/97
1/15/98	1/14/98	1/13/98	1/12/98	1/11/98	1/10/98	1/9/98	1/8/98	1/7/98	1/6/98	1/5/98	1/4/98	1/3/98	1/2/98

Gold Square of Nine – Price (downtrend)

In this chart we set the beginning point at 960, the top of the market, with an increment of –1. The market is falling so we are going down in price. See how the prices support on or near the support lines on the Square of Nine all the way down. This chart example proves that the Square of Nine works just as well in a down trend as in an up trend. Continue to work with the Square of Nine and you will see its effectiveness in all markets.

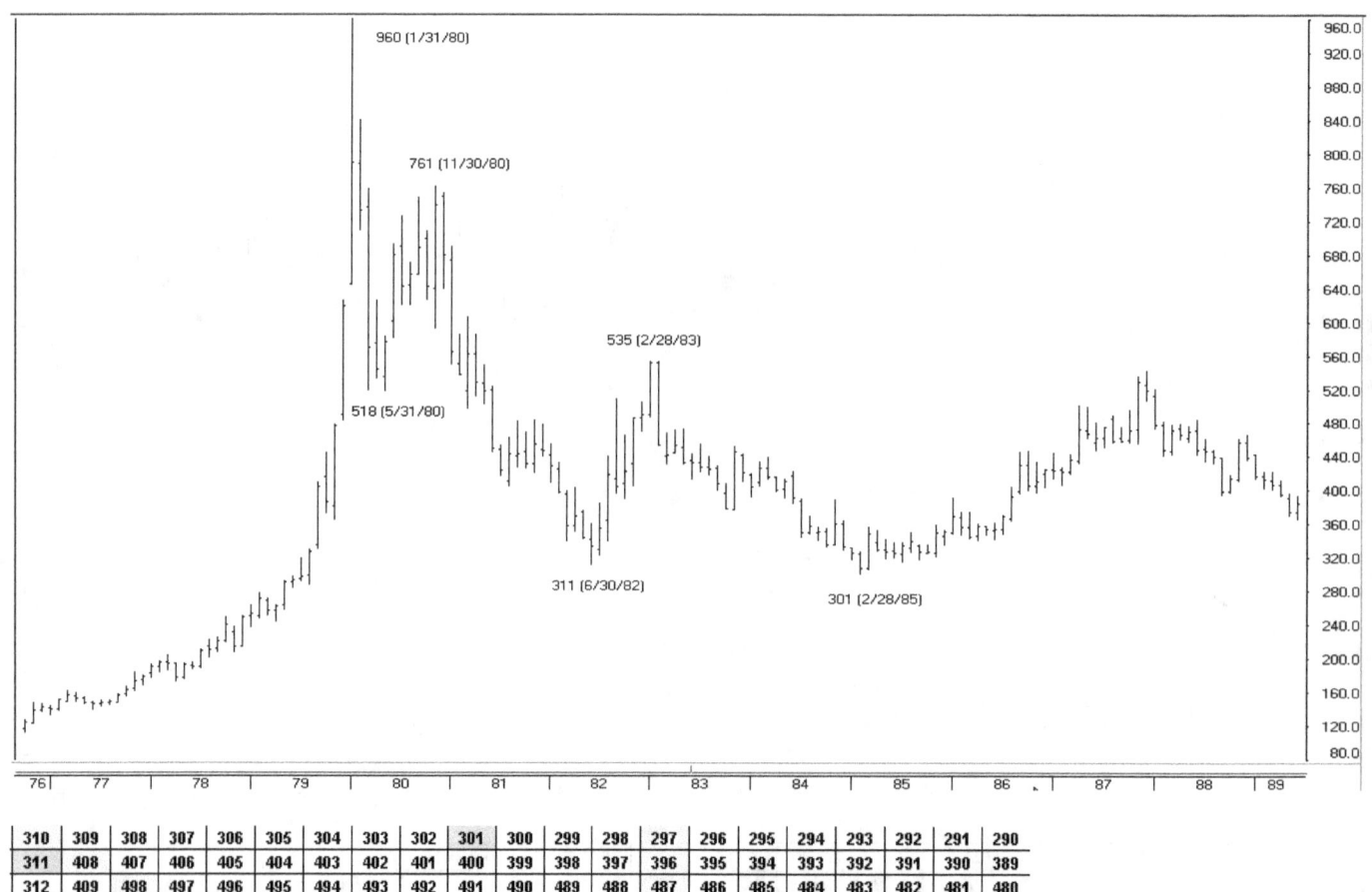

310	309	308	307	306	305	304	303	302	301	300	299	298	297	296	295	294	293	292	291	290
311	408	407	406	405	404	403	402	401	400	399	398	397	396	395	394	393	392	391	390	389
312	409	498	497	496	495	494	493	492	491	490	489	488	487	486	485	484	483	482	481	480
313	410	499	580	579	578	577	576	575	574	573	572	571	570	569	568	567	566	565	564	563
314	411	500	581	654	653	652	651	650	649	648	647	646	645	644	643	642	641	640	639	638
315	412	501	582	655	720	719	718	717	716	715	714	713	712	711	710	709	708	707	706	705
316	413	502	583	656	721	778	777	776	775	774	773	772	771	770	769	768	767	766	765	764
317	414	503	584	657	722	779	828	827	826	825	824	823	822	821	820	819	818	817	816	763
318	415	504	585	658	723	780	829	870	869	868	867	866	865	864	863	862	861	860	815	762
319	416	505	586	659	724	781	830	871	904	903	902	901	900	899	898	897	896	859	814	761
320	417	506	587	660	725	782	831	872	905	930	929	928	927	926	925	924	895	858	813	760
321	418	507	588	661	726	783	832	873	906	931	948	947	946	945	944	923	894	857	812	759
322	419	508	589	662	727	784	833	874	907	932	949	958	957	956	943	922	893	856	811	758
323	420	509	590	663	728	785	834	875	908	933	950	959	960	955	942	921	892	855	810	757
324	421	510	591	664	729	786	835	876	909	934	951	952	953	954	941	920	891	854	809	756
325	422	511	592	665	730	787	836	877	910	935	936	937	938	939	940	919	890	853	808	755
326	423	512	593	666	731	788	837	878	911	912	913	914	915	916	917	918	889	852	807	754
327	424	513	594	667	732	789	838	879	880	881	882	883	884	885	886	887	888	851	806	753
328	425	514	595	668	733	790	839	840	841	842	843	844	845	846	847	848	849	850	805	752
329	426	515	596	669	734	791	792	793	794	795	796	797	798	799	800	801	802	803	804	751
330	427	516	597	670	735	736	737	738	739	740	741	742	743	744	745	746	747	748	749	750
331	428	517	598	671	672	673	674	675	676	677	678	679	680	681	682	683	684	685	686	687
332	429	518	599	600	601	602	603	604	605	606	607	608	609	610	611	612	613	614	615	616
333	430	519	520	521	522	523	524	525	526	527	528	529	530	531	532	533	534	535	536	537

Gold Monthly Time (Downtrend)

In this Gold Monthly time chart we start the chart at the top date of 1/31/80 with an increment of –1 and start down. The Square of Nine gives you the support and resistance points all the way down.

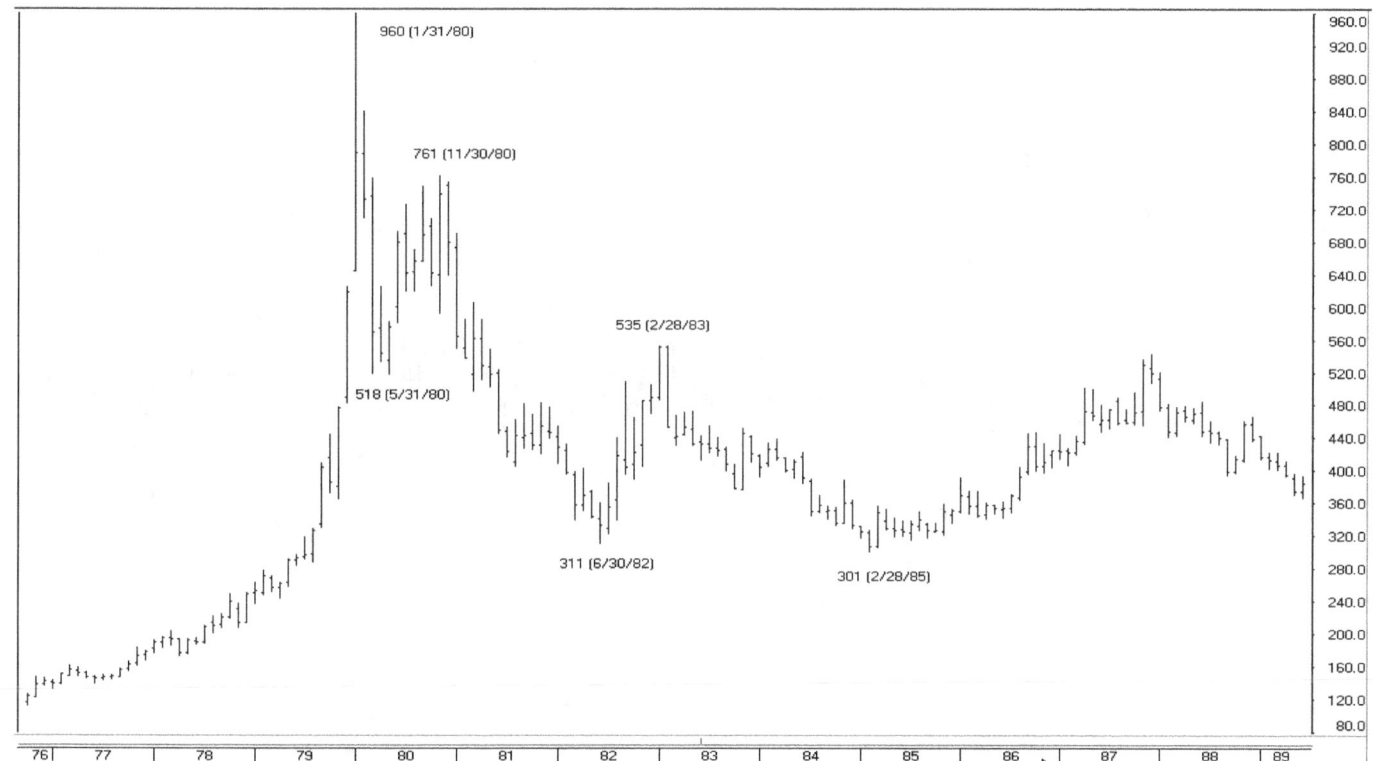

Dec Swiss Franc Monthly Square of Nine – Price Chart

Set the beginning at 3403 and the increment to 5 on this Square of Nine Chart. I have highlighted the highs and the lows on the chart. The highlighted horizontal and diagonal lines on the Square of Nine represent support and resistance. Sometimes the market will stop exactly on these lines and sometimes the market would fail a few squares before the lines. It's amazing how many times the exact tops and bottoms were directly on the support and resistance lines of the Square of Nine.

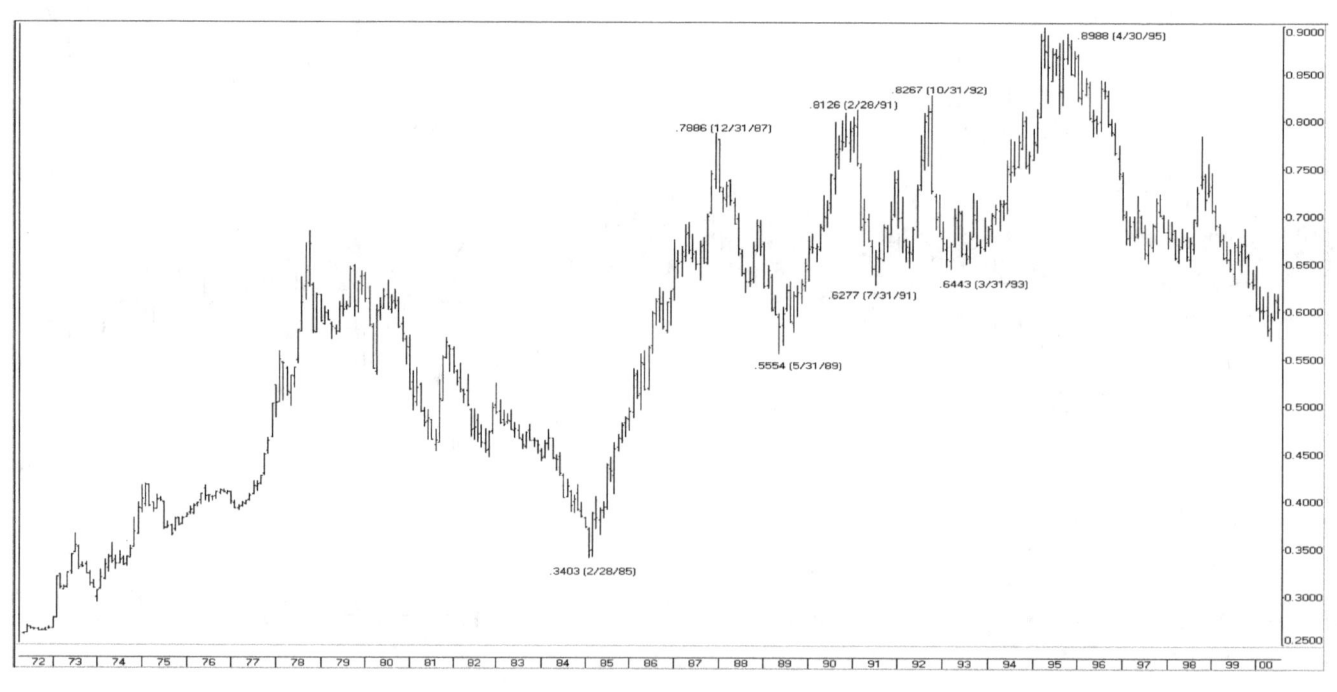

Changing Cells

Because of the size of your computer screen, you may need to change the size of the fonts and the width and height of the squares to make them fit better on your screen. A 19" inch computer screen set to 1280 x 1024 resolution was used to create this book. If you have a smaller or larger screen or difference resolution you may have to make some changes in the settings. You can make these changes by going into your control panel in the computer and making the necessary changes on this display properties screen.

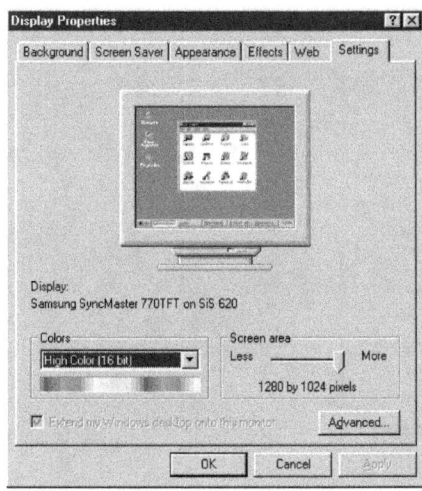

To make changes in Excel you go to format and then to cells…
Set the category to Date for time charts or to Number for price charts.

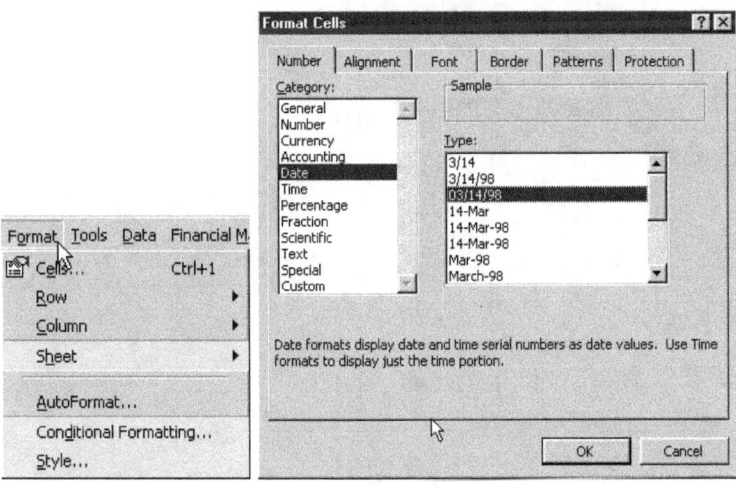

To change the size of the cells to fit your screen go to Format Row.

Then change the Row Height to your desired choice. You must use trial and error to find what fits your screen the best.

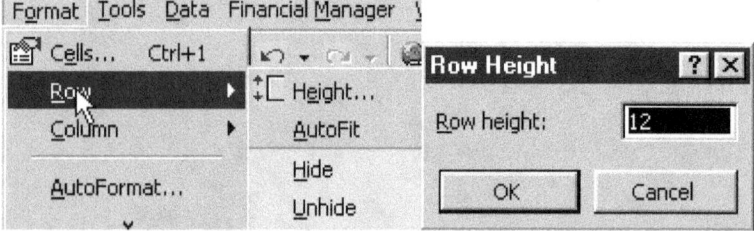

To change the Column Width, go to format column.

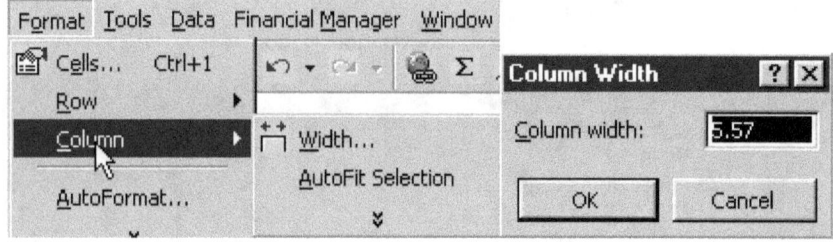

To change fonts and sizes in the cells, highlight the Square of Nine cells by right clicking the mouse and dragging it across the entire area of the Square of Nine, then right click your mouse to format cells in the font section. Change it to your desired font, font style and size. I have found that arial, arial narrow and small fonts work nicely with a 5, 6, 7, or 8 pt. Size.

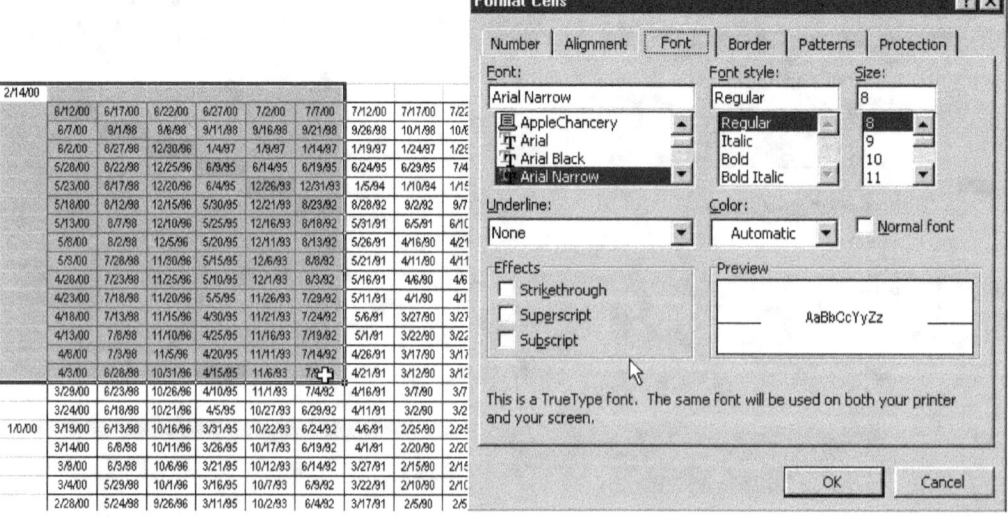

Enlarging the Size of a Chart

If you need to make a chart bigger you can. It takes a little work. Each cell on the chart contains a formula to make it work. For example in the Square of Nine Chart the formula is:

The beginning number plus the increment

[Excel spreadsheet showing a large Square of Nine chart with numbers arranged in rings around a center value of 20, with Begin=20 and Incre=1 labels at the bottom]

In the above Excel example it is:

Begin 20 which is the square of S19.

51	52	53	54	55
32	33	34	35	36
31	22	23	24	37
30	21	20	25	38
29	28	27	26	39
44	43	42	41	40
67	66	65	64	63

Plus the increment of 1, the square of C38.

Begin	20	
Incre	1	
Name		

That square is labeled +R19, which is (+S19+C38).

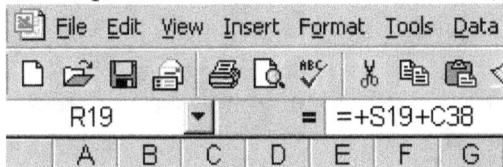

The next square would be R19 + C38 and so on.

Changing a Time Square

It's easy to change your Square of Nine Chart from a price square to a time square. Just go to Format Cells and change the category from Number to Date and Type to 03/14/98.

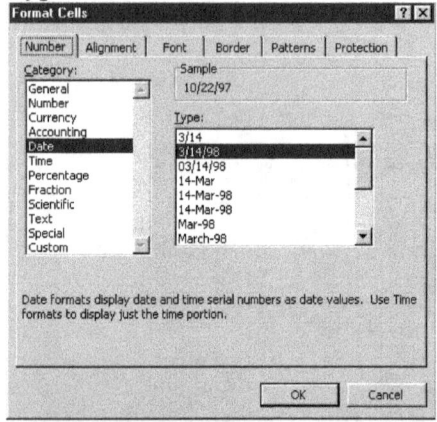

In this example the center is formatted with time.

11/8/96	11/9/96	11/10/96
11/7/96	11/6/96	11/11/96
11/14/96	11/13/96	11/12/96

Begin starts with a time and the increment with a number 1.

Begin	11/6/96
Incre	1

So in the same example as before, using time the first square is R19 which is composed of the center or beginning of S19 + C38.

	A	B	C	D	E	F	G	H	I	J	K	L	M	N	O	P	Q	R	S	T	U
1	2/14/00																		3/30/00		
2		12/3/99	12/4/99	12/5/99	12/6/99	12/7/99	12/8/99	12/9/99	12/10/99	12/11/99	12/12/99	12/13/99	12/14/99	12/15/99	12/16/99	12/17/99	12/18/99	12/19/99	12/20/99	12/21/99	12/22/99
3		12/2/99	7/26/99	7/27/99	7/28/99	7/29/99	7/30/99	7/31/99	8/1/99	8/2/99	8/3/99	8/4/99	8/5/99	8/6/99	8/7/99	8/8/99	8/9/99	8/10/99	8/11/99	8/12/99	8/13/99
4		12/1/99	7/25/99	3/26/99	3/27/99	3/28/99	3/29/99	3/30/99	3/31/99	4/1/99	4/2/99	4/3/99	4/4/99	4/5/99	4/6/99	4/7/99	4/8/99	4/9/99	4/10/99	4/11/99	4/12/99
5		11/30/99	7/24/99	3/25/99	12/2/98	12/3/98	12/4/98	12/5/98	12/6/98	12/7/98	12/8/98	12/9/98	12/10/98	12/11/98	12/12/98	12/13/98	12/14/98	12/15/98	12/16/98	12/17/98	12/18/98
6		11/29/99	7/23/99	3/24/99	12/1/98	8/18/98	8/19/98	8/20/98	8/21/98	8/22/98	8/23/98	8/24/98	8/25/98	8/26/98	8/27/98	8/28/98	8/29/98	8/30/98	8/31/98	9/1/98	9/2/98
7		11/28/99	7/22/99	3/23/99	11/30/98	8/17/98	5/12/98	5/13/98	5/14/98	5/15/98	5/16/98	5/17/98	5/18/98	5/19/98	5/20/98	5/21/98	5/22/98	5/23/98	5/24/98	5/25/98	5/26/98
8		11/27/99	7/21/99	3/22/99	11/29/98	8/16/98	5/11/98	2/11/98	2/12/98	2/13/98	2/14/98	2/15/98	2/16/98	2/17/98	2/18/98	2/19/98	2/20/98	2/21/98	2/22/98	2/23/98	2/24/98
9		11/26/99	7/20/99	3/21/99	11/28/98	8/15/98	5/10/98	2/10/98	11/21/97	11/22/97	11/23/97	11/24/97	11/25/97	11/26/97	11/27/97	11/28/97	11/29/97	11/30/97	12/1/97	12/2/97	12/3/97
10		11/25/99	7/19/99	3/20/99	11/27/98	8/14/98	5/9/98	2/9/98	11/20/97	9/8/97	9/9/97	9/10/97	9/11/97	9/12/97	9/13/97	9/14/97	9/15/97	9/16/97	9/17/97	9/18/97	9/19/97
11		11/24/99	7/18/99	3/19/99	11/26/98	8/13/98	5/8/98	2/8/98	11/19/97	9/7/97	7/4/97	7/5/97	7/6/97	7/7/97	7/8/97	7/9/97	7/10/97	7/11/97	7/12/97	7/13/97	7/14/97
12		11/23/99	7/17/99	3/18/99	11/25/98	8/12/98	5/7/98	2/7/98	11/18/97	9/6/97	7/3/97	5/7/97	5/8/97	5/9/97	5/10/97	5/11/97	5/12/97	5/13/97	5/14/97	5/15/97	5/16/97
13		11/22/99	7/16/99	3/17/99	11/24/98	8/11/98	5/6/98	2/6/98	11/17/97	9/5/97	7/2/97	5/6/97	3/16/97	3/19/97	3/20/97	3/21/97	3/22/97	3/23/97	3/24/97	3/25/97	3/26/97
14		11/21/99	7/15/99	3/16/99	11/23/98	8/10/98	5/5/98	2/5/98	11/16/97	9/4/97	7/1/97	5/5/97	3/17/97	2/4/97	2/5/97	2/6/97	2/7/97	2/8/97	2/9/97	2/10/97	2/11/97
15		11/20/99	7/14/99	3/15/99	11/22/98	8/9/98	5/4/98	2/4/98	11/15/97	9/3/97	6/30/97	5/4/97	3/16/97	2/3/97	1/1/97	1/2/97	1/3/97	1/4/97	1/5/97	1/6/97	1/7/97
16		11/19/99	7/13/99	3/14/99	11/21/98	8/8/98	5/3/98	2/3/98	11/14/97	9/2/97	6/29/97	5/3/97	3/15/97	2/2/97	12/31/96	12/5/96	12/7/96	12/8/96	12/9/96	12/10/96	12/11/96
17		11/18/99	7/12/99	3/13/99	11/20/98	8/7/98	5/2/98	2/2/98	11/13/97	9/1/97	6/28/97	5/2/97	3/14/97	2/1/97	12/30/96	12/5/96	11/18/96	11/19/96	11/20/96	11/21/96	11/22/96
18		11/17/99	7/11/99	3/12/99	11/19/98	8/6/98	5/1/98	2/1/98	11/12/97	8/31/97	6/27/97	5/1/97	3/13/97	1/31/97	12/29/96	12/4/96	11/17/96	11/8/96	11/9/96	11/10/96	11/23/96
19	1/0/00	11/16/99	7/10/99	3/11/99	11/18/98	8/5/98	4/30/98	1/31/98	11/11/97	8/30/97	6/26/97	4/30/97	3/12/97	1/30/97	12/28/96	12/3/96	11/16/96	11/7/96	11/6/96	11/11/96	11/24/96
20		11/15/99	7/9/99	3/10/99	11/17/98	8/4/98	4/29/98	1/30/98	11/10/97	8/29/97	6/25/97	4/29/97	3/11/97	1/29/97	12/27/96	12/2/96	11/15/96	11/14/96	11/13/96	11/12/96	11/25/96
21		11/14/99	7/8/99	3/9/99	11/16/98	8/3/98	4/28/98	1/29/98	11/9/97	8/28/97	6/24/97	4/28/97	3/10/97	1/28/97	12/26/96	12/1/96	11/30/96	11/29/96	11/28/96	11/27/96	11/26/96
22		11/13/99	7/7/99	3/8/99	11/15/98	8/2/98	4/27/98	1/28/98	11/8/97	8/27/97	6/23/97	4/27/97	3/9/97	1/27/97	12/25/96	12/24/96	12/23/96	12/22/96	12/21/96	12/20/96	12/19/96
23		11/12/99	7/6/99	3/7/99	11/14/98	8/1/98	4/26/98	1/27/98	11/7/97	8/26/97	6/22/97	4/26/97	3/8/97	1/26/97	1/25/97	1/24/97	1/23/97	1/22/97	1/21/97	1/20/97	1/19/97
24		11/11/99	7/5/99	3/6/99	11/13/98	7/31/98	4/25/98	1/26/98	11/6/97	8/25/97	6/21/97	4/25/97	3/7/97	3/6/97	3/5/97	3/4/97	3/3/97	3/2/97	3/1/97	2/28/97	2/27/97
25		11/10/99	7/4/99	3/5/99	11/12/98	7/30/98	4/24/98	1/25/98	11/5/97	8/24/97	6/20/97	4/24/97	4/23/97	4/22/97	4/21/97	4/20/97	4/19/97	4/18/97	4/17/97	4/16/97	4/15/97
26		11/9/99	7/3/99	3/4/99	11/11/98	7/29/98	4/23/98	1/24/98	11/4/97	8/23/97	6/19/97	6/18/97	6/17/97	6/16/97	6/15/97	6/14/97	6/13/97	6/12/97	6/11/97	6/10/97	6/9/97
27		11/8/99	7/2/99	3/3/99	11/10/98	7/28/98	4/22/98	1/23/98	11/3/97	8/22/97	8/21/97	8/20/97	8/19/97	8/18/97	8/17/97	8/16/97	8/15/97	8/14/97	8/13/97	8/12/97	8/11/97
28		11/7/99	7/1/99	3/2/99	11/9/98	7/27/98	4/21/98	1/22/98	11/2/97	11/1/97	10/31/97	10/30/97	10/29/97	10/28/97	10/27/97	10/26/97	10/25/97	10/24/97	10/23/97	10/22/97	10/21/97
29		11/6/99	6/30/99	3/1/99	11/8/98	7/26/98	4/20/98	1/21/98	1/20/98	1/19/98	1/18/98	1/17/98	1/16/98	1/15/98	1/14/98	1/13/98	1/12/98	1/11/98	1/10/98	1/9/98	1/8/98
30		11/5/99	6/29/99	2/28/99	11/7/98	7/25/98	4/19/98	4/18/98	4/17/98	4/16/98	4/15/98	4/14/98	4/13/98	4/12/98	4/11/98	4/10/98	4/9/98	4/8/98	4/7/98	4/6/98	4/5/98
31		11/4/99	6/28/99	2/27/99	11/6/98	7/24/98	7/23/98	7/22/98	7/21/98	7/20/98	7/19/98	7/18/98	7/17/98	7/16/98	7/15/98	7/14/98	7/13/98	7/12/98	7/11/98	7/10/98	7/9/98
32		11/3/99	6/27/99	2/26/99	11/5/98	11/4/98	11/3/98	11/2/98	11/1/98	10/31/98	10/30/98	10/29/98	10/28/98	10/27/98	10/26/98	10/25/98	10/24/98	10/23/98	10/22/98	10/21/98	10/20/98
33		11/2/99	6/26/99	2/25/99	2/24/99	2/23/99	2/22/99	2/21/99	2/20/99	2/19/99	2/18/99	2/17/99	2/16/99	2/15/99	2/14/99	2/13/99	2/12/99	2/11/99	2/10/99	2/9/99	2/8/99
34		11/1/99	6/25/99	6/24/99	6/23/99	6/22/99	6/21/99	6/20/99	6/19/99	6/18/99	6/17/99	6/16/99	6/15/99	6/14/99	6/13/99	6/12/99	6/11/99	6/10/99	6/9/99	6/8/99	6/7/99
35		10/31/99	10/30/99	10/29/99	10/28/99	10/27/99	10/26/99	10/25/99	10/24/99	10/23/99	10/22/99	10/21/99	10/20/99	10/19/99	10/18/99	10/17/99	10/16/99	10/15/99	10/14/99	10/13/99	10/12/99
36	11/10/00	3/14/00	3/13/00	3/12/00	3/11/00	3/10/00	3/9/00	3/8/00	3/7/00	3/6/00	3/5/00	3/4/00	3/3/00	3/2/00	3/1/00	2/29/00	2/28/00	2/27/00	2/26/00	2/25/00	2/24/00
37		Begin	11/6/96																		
38		Incre	1																		

In all the various formats you would take the previous square and add the increment in the direction of the chart. You can enlarge any chart to any size you want, with some work.

Swiss Franc Monthly Square of Nine – Time Chart

In this chart the time was set to 2/1/85 and the increment to 5. The highs and lows were highlighted. Notice how many of these points hit the resistance and support levels. Only in two times were they off by a couple squares. You will find that in most cases the monthly charts work better the weekly charts and the weekly charts work better than daily charts using the Square of Nine. That's because there is more interference with shorter-term markets.

Chapter 3
Square of Four

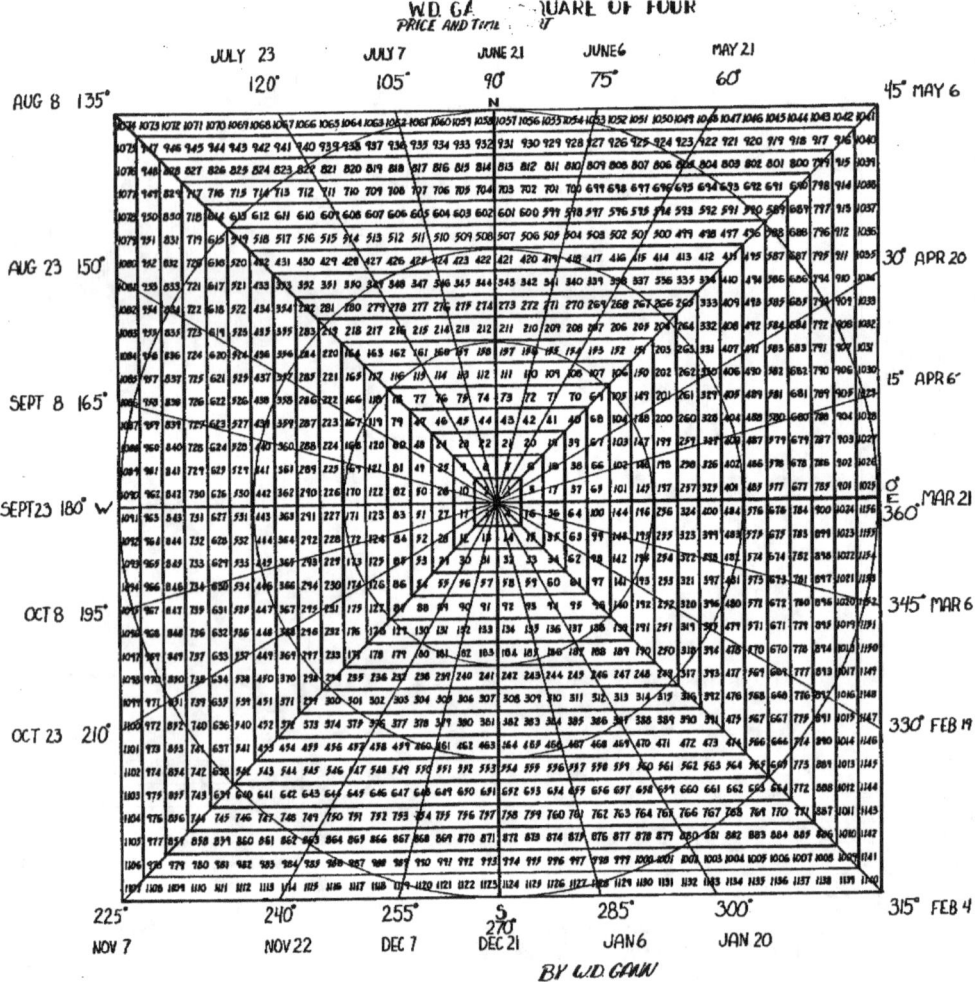

This is Gann's Square of Four, which he used in many of his calculations. The numbers are hand-drawn and the lines and circles are drawn with a compass and protractor by Gann. Now the question is, which square should you use, the Square of Four or the Square of Nine. Consideration should be given as to what fits best. Check the trading pattern to see if it fits the Square of Nine or the Square of Four. Sometimes it has to do with the number of trading days in the contract in respect to commodities. If you know the complete number of trading days for a contract, you can map them out in the squares. Then determine the starting days and see if the commodity prices are following the dates on the sides of the Square of Nine or Square of Four.

Gann's Example and Use of Square of Four

Here is an example of a Square of Four Chart used by Gann in actual calculations. He started the square with 330 with an increment of 30. This was for March Coffee. He divided the chart up into angle divisions for the year with corresponding dates on the outer rim. You will find that in many cases the outer dates and the inside prices will correspond with each other. You will find that the price of the market will be on the exact date at the same time during the year in many cases.

Gann's Example and Use of the Square of Four – May Coffee

Here is another example of the use of the Square of Four Chart by Gann. He started the chart at 570, which was a low with an increment of 30 just like he did in the previous example. The outside parameter of the chart is also labeled with calendar dates. As you can see Gann put a lot of work in these charts and therefore you should not overlook the importance of doing your homework with them also.

Gann's Master Price of Time Chart – Square of Four

Here is another example of the Square of Four Chart, which Gann used to trade cotton, coffee, cocoa, and grains. This was his master chart, which he set at 12 at the beginning with an increment of 12. There are 24 hours in a day and 12 months in a year. He set the outer parameter to calendar dates of the year.

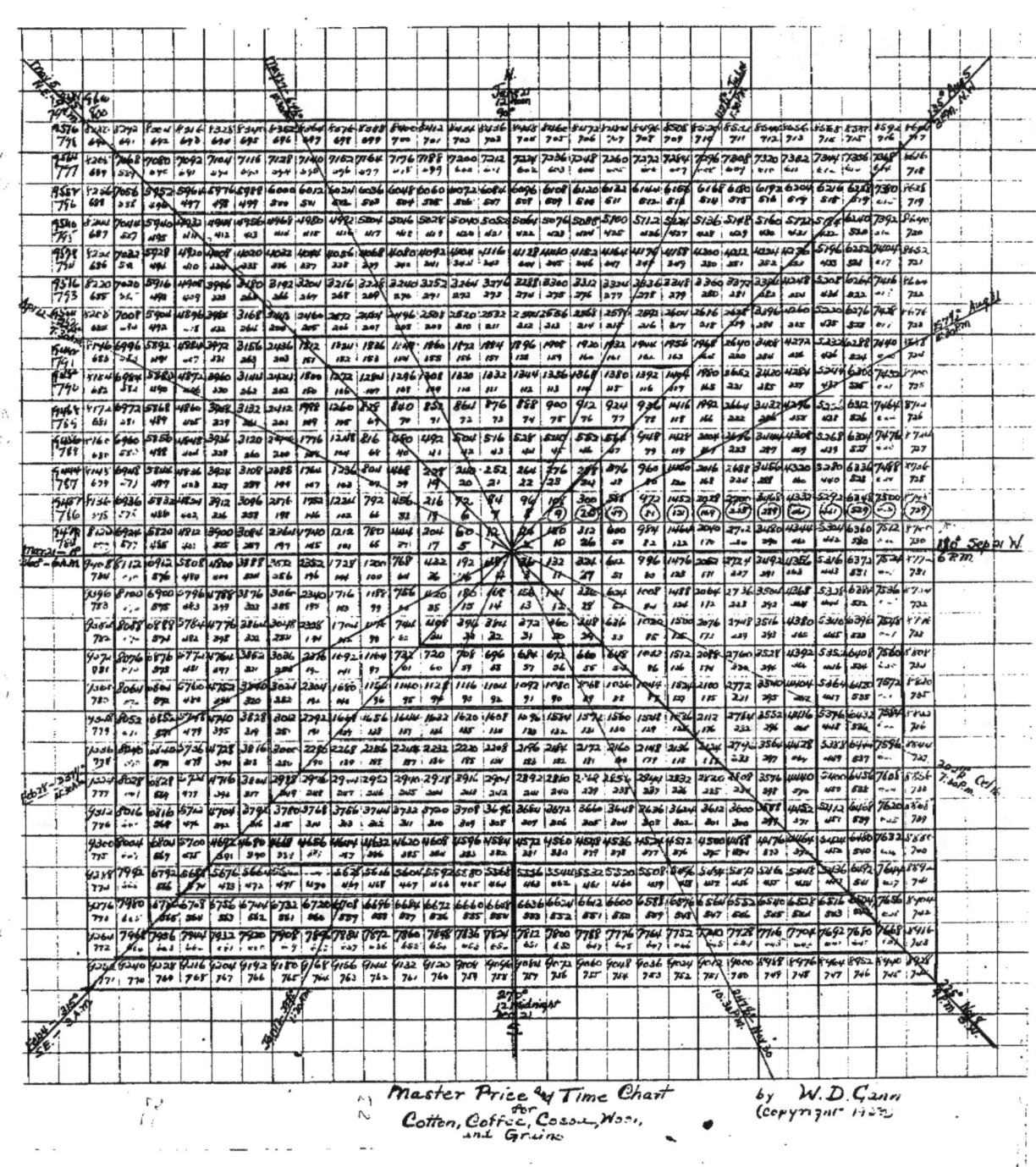

Chapter 4
Gann's Ratio Calculator

One of Gann's methods, which is not talked about very much, is his ratio calculator. It used to be very difficult to calculate, but now it is very easy using the Excel template in this book. Gann's Ratio Calculator will tell you where the price move might go.

Here's how to use it. First determine the starting price, which is either a top or a bottom. Divide that price by the days in the time movement. For example, the first day is 1. So you just divide the first day's price by 1, which gives you a ratio.

You then project these figures out and when you get a ratio, which is a harmonic of the original price you have a projection of where it is going to stop. If it gets through one harmonic number, then it will usually go to the next harmonic number. What I mean by a harmonic number is, in the wheat example 4.02 is a harmonic of 402. The half number of 201 and 101 ½ are also harmonics. The market should stop at most of these harmonic numbers.

In this chapter we used two examples. One example is Dec Wheat in an uptrend and the second example is a stock, A.G. Edwards in a downtrend.

Work with this ratio calculator using historical data and you will see how nicely it works.

Remember you can take this Ratio Chart out further than it is already buy expanding it according to the techniques of using the Excel program.

Also remember that this calculator method should be combined with other trading techniques to increase its effectiveness. Gann said that the more things hitting at one point, the more significant it is.

Gann Ratio Calculator – Dec Wheat

The Ratio calculator is an excellent tool to tell you where a market might go. In this example the market started at 402 on December Wheat. Set the Beginning price at 402 and watch the ratio. When the ratio hits a harmonic of the original price, in this case it was 4.02, check the price column and that is where it should stop. In this case it was at 547. Notice that here the market was so strong that it went through the 547 level, but then finally fell back and started a major correction.

PRICE	/ TIME	= RATIO	PRICE	/ TIME	= RATIO	PRICE	/ TIME	= RATIO	PRICE	/ TIME	= RATIO	PRICE	/ TIME	= RATIO
402	1	402	432	31	13.93548	462	61	7.57377	492	91	5.406593	522	111	4.702703
403	2	201.5	433	32	13.53125	463	62	7.467742	493	92	5.358696	523	112	4.669643
404	3	134.6667	434	33	13.15152	464	63	7.365079	494	93	5.311828	524	113	4.637168
405	4	101.25	435	34	12.79412	465	64	7.265625	495	94	5.265957	525	114	4.605263
406	5	81.2	436	35	12.45714	466	65	7.169231	496	95	5.221053	526	115	4.573913
407	6	67.83333	437	36	12.13889	467	66	7.075758	497	96	5.177083	527	116	4.543103
408	7	58.28571	438	37	11.83784	468	67	6.985075	498	97	5.134021	528	117	4.512821
409	8	51.125	439	38	11.55263	469	68	6.897059	499	98	5.091837	529	118	4.483051
410	9	45.55556	440	39	11.28205	470	69	6.811594	500	99	5.050505	530	119	4.453782
411	10	41.1	441	40	11.025	471	70	6.728571	501	100	5.01	531	120	4.425
412	11	37.45455	442	41	10.78049	472	71	6.647887	502	101	4.970297	532	121	4.396694
413	12	34.41667	443	42	10.54762	473	72	6.569444	503	102	4.931373	533	122	4.368852
414	13	31.84615	444	43	10.32558	474	73	6.493151	504	103	4.893204	534	123	4.341463
415	14	29.64286	445	44	10.11364	475	74	6.418919	505	104	4.855769	535	124	4.314516
416	15	27.73333	446	45	9.911111	476	75	6.346667	506	105	4.819048	536	125	4.288
417	16	26.0625	447	46	9.717391	477	76	6.276316	507	106	4.783019	537	126	4.261905
418	17	24.58824	448	47	9.531915	478	77	6.207792	508	107	4.747664	538	127	4.23622
419	18	23.27778	449	48	9.354167	479	78	6.141026	509	108	4.712963	539	128	4.210938
420	19	22.10526	450	49	9.183673	480	79	6.075949	510	109	4.678899	540	129	4.186047
421	20	21.05	451	50	9.02	481	80	6.0125	511	110	4.645455	541	130	4.161538
422	21	20.09524	452	51	8.862745	482	81	5.950617	512	111	4.612613	542	131	4.137405
423	22	19.22727	453	52	8.711538	483	82	5.890244	513	112	4.580357	543	132	4.113636
424	23	18.43478	454	53	8.566038	484	83	5.831325	514	113	4.548673	544	133	4.090226
425	24	17.70833	455	54	8.425926	485	84	5.77381	515	114	4.517544	545	134	4.067164
426	25	17.04	456	55	8.290909	486	85	5.717647	516	115	4.486957	546	135	4.044444
427	26	16.42308	457	56	8.160714	487	86	5.662791	517	116	4.456897	547	136	4.022059
428	27	15.85185	458	57	8.035088	488	87	5.609195	518	117	4.42735	548	137	4
429	28	15.32143	459	58	7.913793	489	88	5.556818	519	118	4.398305	549	138	3.978261
430	29	14.82759	460	59	7.79661	490	89	5.505618	520	119	4.369748	550	139	3.956835
431	30	14.36667	461	60	7.683333	491	90	5.455556	521	110	4.736364	551	140	3.935714

Begin	402
Incre	1
Name	DEC WHEAT

Gann's Ratio Calculator – A.G. Edwards

You can also use the Ratio Chart to tell you where a stock or commodity might go in a downtrend. In this case A.G. Edwards topped at 38. So we put 38 in the beginning box. The increment was put in at -.2. When the ratio went to 1.89394 38 (38/10=3.8/2=1.9) it was a major bottom.

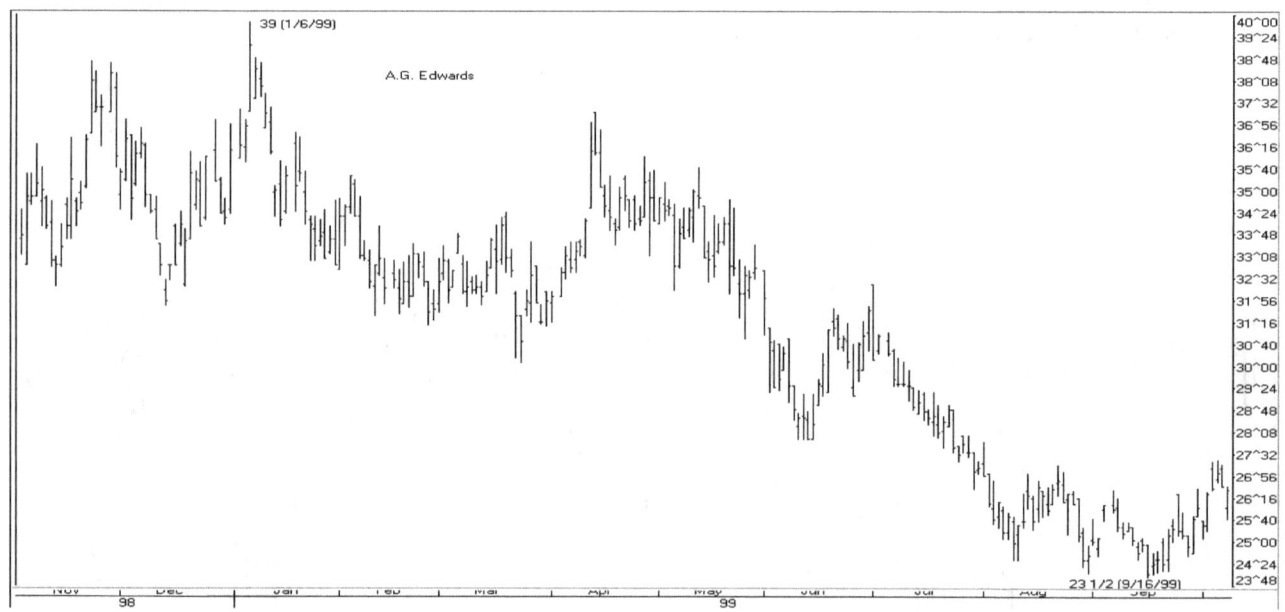

PRICE	/ TIME	= RATIO	PRICE	/ TIME	= RATIO	PRICE	/ TIME	= RATIO	PRICE	/ TIME	= RATIO	PRICE	/ TIME	= RATIO	PRICE	/ TIME	= RATIO
38	-0.2	-190	32	-6.2	-5.16129	26	-12.2	-2.13115	20	-18.2	-1.0989	14	-22.2	-0.63063	8	-28.2	-0.28369
37.8	-0.4	-94.5	31.8	-6.4	-4.96875	25.8	-12.4	-2.08065	19.8	-18.4	-1.07609	13.8	-22.4	-0.61607	7.8	-28.4	-0.27465
37.6	-0.6	-62.6667	31.6	-6.6	-4.78788	25.6	-12.6	-2.03175	19.6	-18.6	-1.05376	13.6	-22.6	-0.60177	7.6	-28.6	-0.26573
37.4	-0.8	-46.75	31.4	-6.8	-4.61765	25.4	-12.8	-1.98438	19.4	-18.8	-1.03191	13.4	-22.8	-0.58772	7.4	-28.8	-0.25694
37.2	-1	-37.2	31.2	-7	-4.45714	25.2	-13	-1.93846	19.2	-19	-1.01053	13.2	-23	-0.57391	7.2	-29	-0.24828
37	-1.2	-30.8333	31	-7.2	-4.30556	25	-13.2	-1.89394	19	-19.2	-0.98958	13	-23.2	-0.56034	7	-29.2	-0.23973
36.8	-1.4	-26.2857	30.8	-7.4	-4.16216	24.8	-13.4	-1.85075	18.8	-19.4	-0.96907	12.8	-23.4	-0.54701	6.8	-29.4	-0.23129
36.6	-1.6	-22.875	30.6	-7.6	-4.02632	24.6	-13.6	-1.80882	18.6	-19.6	-0.94898	12.6	-23.6	-0.5339	6.6	-29.6	-0.22297
36.4	-1.8	-20.2222	30.4	-7.8	-3.89744	24.4	-13.8	-1.76812	18.4	-19.8	-0.92929	12.4	-23.8	-0.52101	6.4	-29.8	-0.21477
36.2	-2	-18.1	30.2	-8	-3.775	24.2	-14	-1.72857	18.2	-20	-0.91	12.2	-24	-0.50833	6.2	-30	-0.20667
36	-2.2	-16.3636	30	-8.2	-3.65854	24	-14.2	-1.69014	18	-20.2	-0.89109	12	-24.2	-0.49587	6	-30.2	-0.19868
35.8	-2.4	-14.9167	29.8	-8.4	-3.54762	23.8	-14.4	-1.65278	17.8	-20.4	-0.87255	11.8	-24.4	-0.48361	5.8	-30.4	-0.19079
35.6	-2.6	-13.6923	29.6	-8.6	-3.44186	23.6	-14.6	-1.61644	17.6	-20.6	-0.85437	11.6	-24.6	-0.47154	5.6	-30.6	-0.18301
35.4	-2.8	-12.6429	29.4	-8.8	-3.34091	23.4	-14.8	-1.58108	17.4	-20.8	-0.83654	11.4	-24.8	-0.45968	5.4	-30.8	-0.17532
35.2	-3	-11.7333	29.2	-9	-3.24444	23.2	-15	-1.54667	17.2	-21	-0.81905	11.2	-25	-0.448	5.2	-31	-0.16774
35	-3.2	-10.9375	29	-9.2	-3.15217	23	-15.2	-1.51316	17	-21.2	-0.80189	11	-25.2	-0.43651	5	-31.2	-0.16026
34.8	-3.4	-10.2353	28.8	-9.4	-3.06383	22.8	-15.4	-1.48052	16.8	-21.4	-0.78505	10.8	-25.4	-0.4252	4.8	-31.4	-0.15287
34.6	-3.6	-9.61111	28.6	-9.6	-2.97917	22.6	-15.6	-1.44872	16.6	-21.6	-0.76852	10.6	-25.6	-0.41406	4.6	-31.6	-0.14557
34.4	-3.8	-9.05263	28.4	-9.8	-2.89796	22.4	-15.8	-1.41772	16.4	-21.8	-0.75229	10.4	-25.8	-0.4031	4.4	-31.8	-0.13836
34.2	-4	-8.55	28.2	-10	-2.82	22.2	-16	-1.3875	16.2	-22	-0.73636	10.2	-26	-0.39231	4.2	-32	-0.13125
34	-4.2	-8.09524	28	-10.2	-2.7451	22	-16.2	-1.35802	16	-22.2	-0.72072	10	-26.2	-0.38168	4	-32.2	-0.12422
33.8	-4.4	-7.68182	27.8	-10.4	-2.67308	21.8	-16.4	-1.32927	15.8	-22.4	-0.70536	9.8	-26.4	-0.37121	3.8	-32.4	-0.11728
33.6	-4.6	-7.30435	27.6	-10.6	-2.60377	21.6	-16.6	-1.3012	15.6	-22.6	-0.69027	9.6	-26.6	-0.3609	3.6	-32.6	-0.11043
33.4	-4.8	-6.95833	27.4	-10.8	-2.53704	21.4	-16.8	-1.27381	15.4	-22.8	-0.67544	9.4	-26.8	-0.35075	3.4	-32.8	-0.10366
33.2	-5	-6.64	27.2	-11	-2.47273	21.2	-17	-1.24706	15.2	-23	-0.66087	9.2	-27	-0.34074	3.2	-33	-0.09697
33	-5.2	-6.34615	27	-11.2	-2.41071	21	-17.2	-1.22093	15	-23.2	-0.64655	9	-27.2	-0.33088	3	-33.2	-0.09036
32.8	-5.4	-6.07407	26.8	-11.4	-2.35088	20.8	-17.4	-1.1954	14.8	-23.4	-0.63248	8.8	-27.4	-0.32117	2.8	-33.4	-0.08383
32.6	-5.6	-5.82143	26.6	-11.6	-2.2931	20.6	-17.6	-1.17045	14.6	-23.6	-0.61864	8.6	-27.6	-0.31159	2.6	-33.6	-0.07738
32.4	-5.8	-5.58621	26.4	-11.8	-2.23729	20.4	-17.8	-1.14607	14.4	-23.8	-0.60504	8.4	-27.8	-0.30216	2.4	-33.8	-0.07101
32.2	-6	-5.36667	26.2	-12	-2.18333	20.2	-18	-1.12222	14.2	-22	-0.64545	8.2	-28	-0.29286	2.2	-34	-0.06471

Begin	38
Incre	-0.2
Name	A.G. Edwards

Chapter 5
Gann's Hexagon Chart

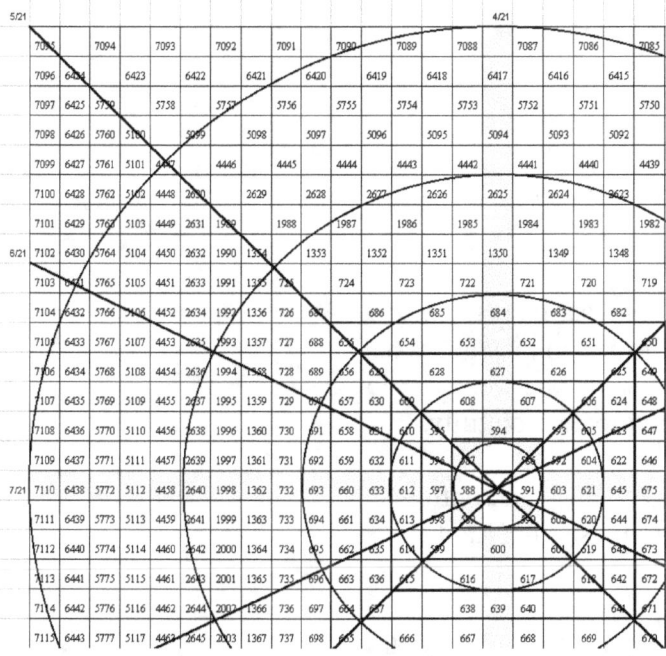

Please note in the above chart I have zoomed it at 200%

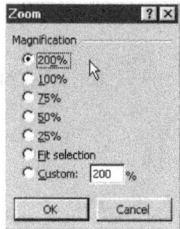

The Hexagon Chart is an important chart that Gann's used in his trading of the markets. The chart has 12 zones, each represents 30 degrees of the circle or a total of 360 degrees. The chart starts at zero and increases anti-clockwise 30 degrees in every zone. Gann used it to forecast support and resistance time and price points.

The center starts at 0. The first level starts with 2 and goes out to 6. It has six numbers in its level. The second level starts with 7 and goes out to 18. It has 12 numbers in it. Each level increases the numbers inside of it by 6. The chart represents the 360 divisions of the year. One complete cycle around the hexagon is, of course, equal to 1 full year. The year starts with the Equinox (Spring). The beginning, which starts with the beginning of spring is labeled as 3/21 and goes all around the circle ending with 2/21. It divides the year into 12 different parts.

3/21
4/21
5/21
6/21
7/21
8/21
9/21
10/21
11/21
12/21
1/21
2/21

Gann said that this chart is used to illustrate to you how angles affect stocks at low and high levels. He said the stocks move faster the further up they go. What has happened when a stock gets high in price is that the distance between the 45 degree angles gets wider and stocks swing faster and with greater volatility.

Gann said that everything is looking for the center of gravity. Top and bottoms are made according to the centers and measurements from these important centers. The hexagon clearly illustrated this.

You can also put the degrees of the circle of 360 and calendar dates of the year around the parameter of the Hexagon Chart. It's very easy to do in the Excel program. These dates will often times coincide with the prices inside the Hexagon Chart.

Hexagon Time Chart - November Soybeans

If you use the fixed method keeping the beginning at 3/21 and the increment at 1 you will see that many turns occur around the 12 divisions of the year. Check out this Soybean chart with the turns that occurred around the 12 hexagon division points of the year.

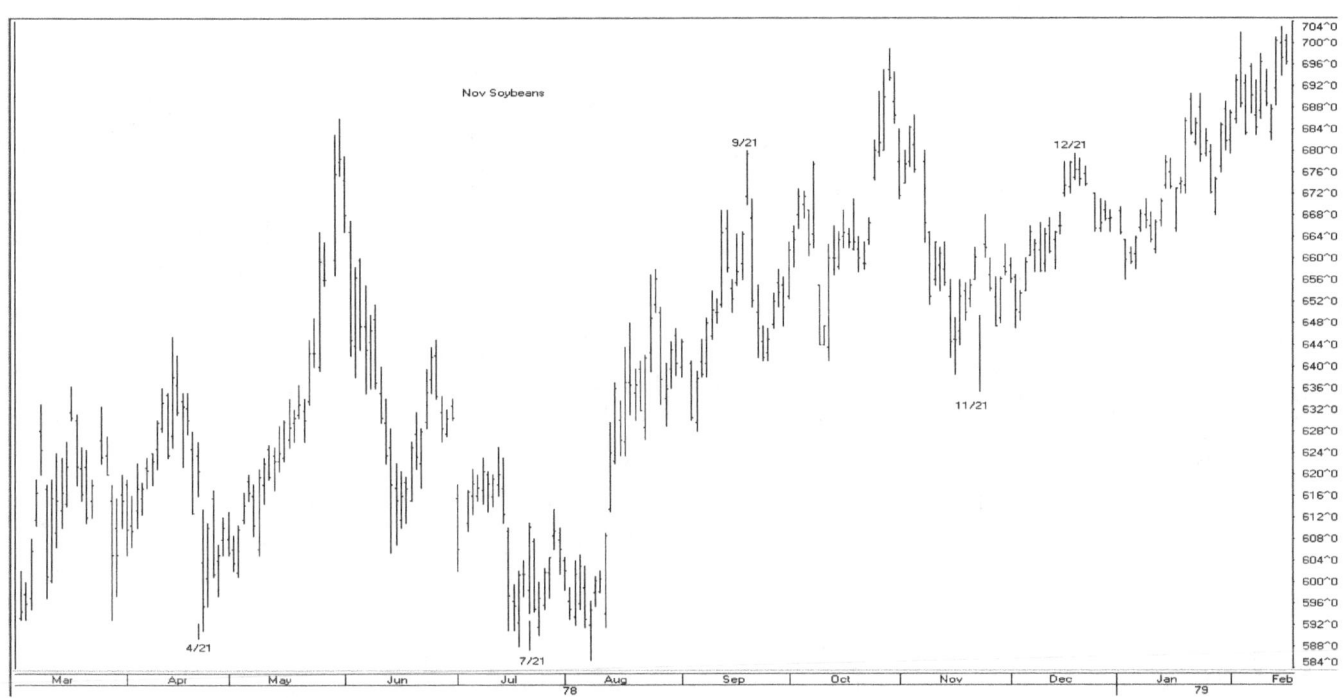

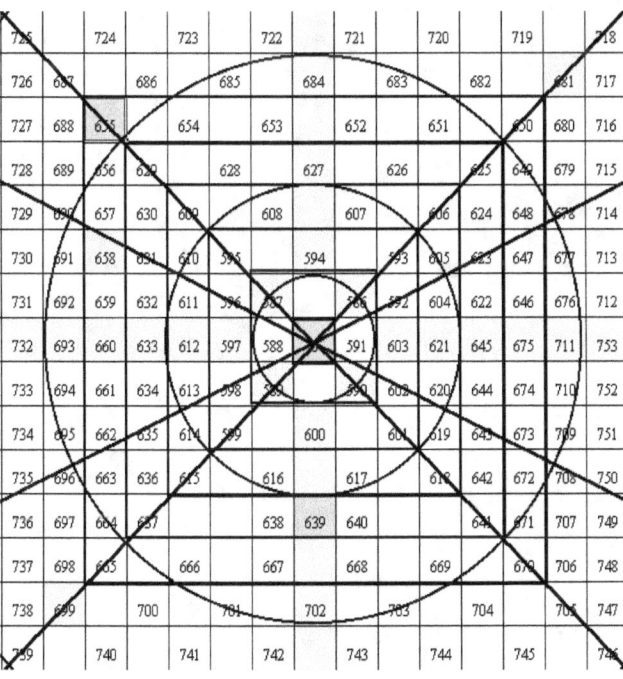

Hexagon Price Chart - November Soybeans

If we take our Hexagon Chart and begin it at 586 with an increment of 1, you will find that most of the highs and lows occurred almost exactly on the 12 division lines of the chart. Notice the highlighted highs and lows.

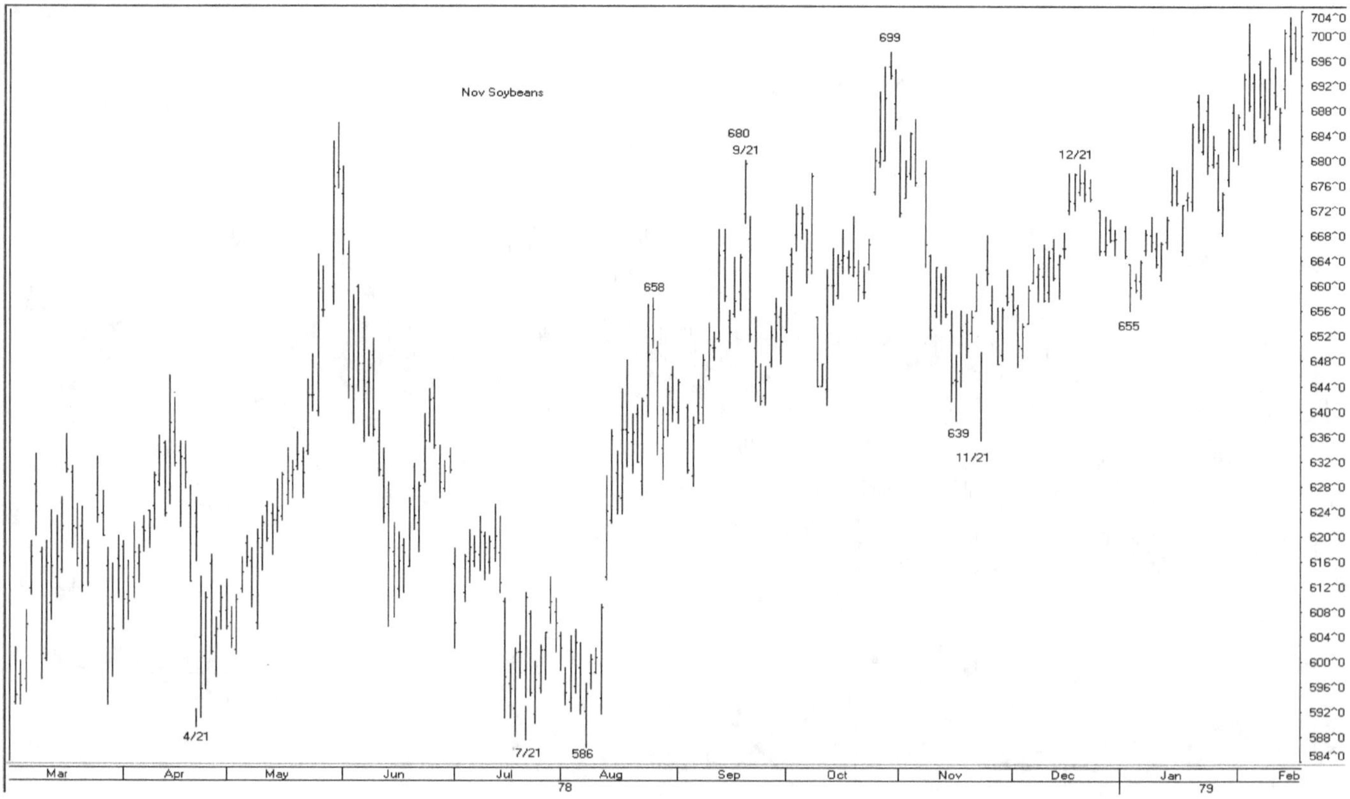

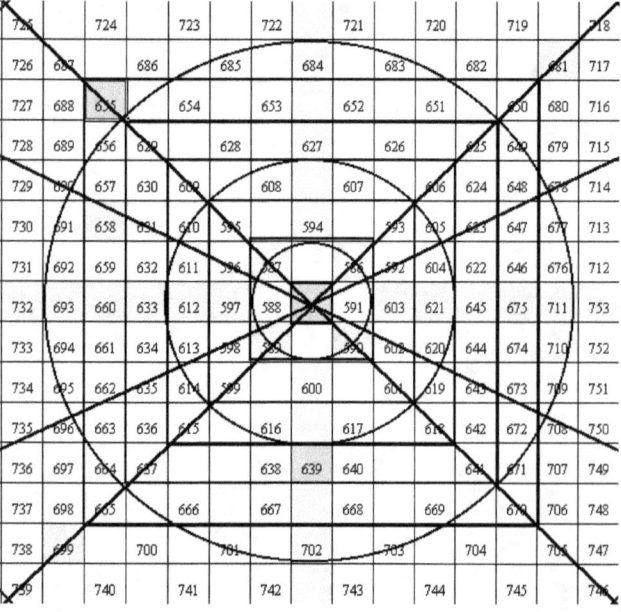

Hexagon Time Chart - November Soybeans

In this example, we converted the Hexagon Price Chart to a Hexagon Time Chart using 8/7/79 for the low and 1 for increment. Notice how many of the time reversals occurred exactly on one of the 12 angles of the hexagon chart.

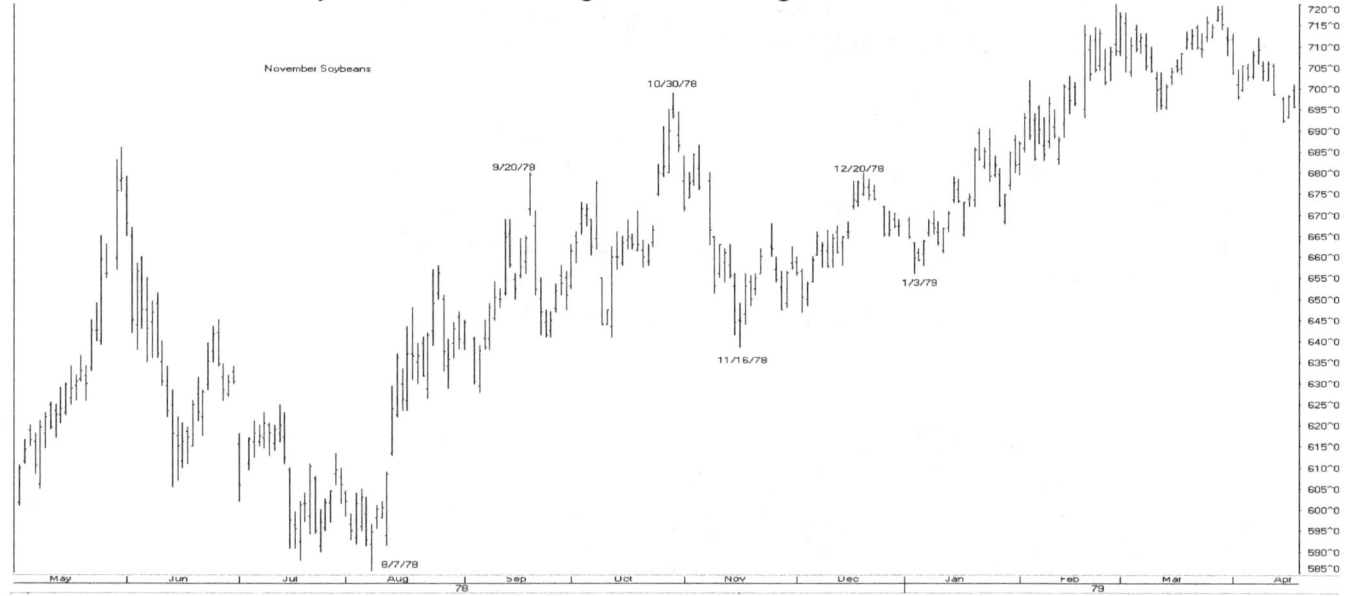

Chapter 6
Gann's Circle Charts

Here is an example of Gann's Circle Chart of 24. This divides the year into 24 parts. See the calendar dates on the parameter of the chart. There are 12 months in a year and 24 hours in a day. Gann used the inside triangle and square in this circle to get the even and odd divisions of the circle. The inside square is used to divide the circle up into 4 parts and the triangle divides it up into 3 parts. You will find the many support and resistance points fall on either the square or the triangle division lines of the circle.

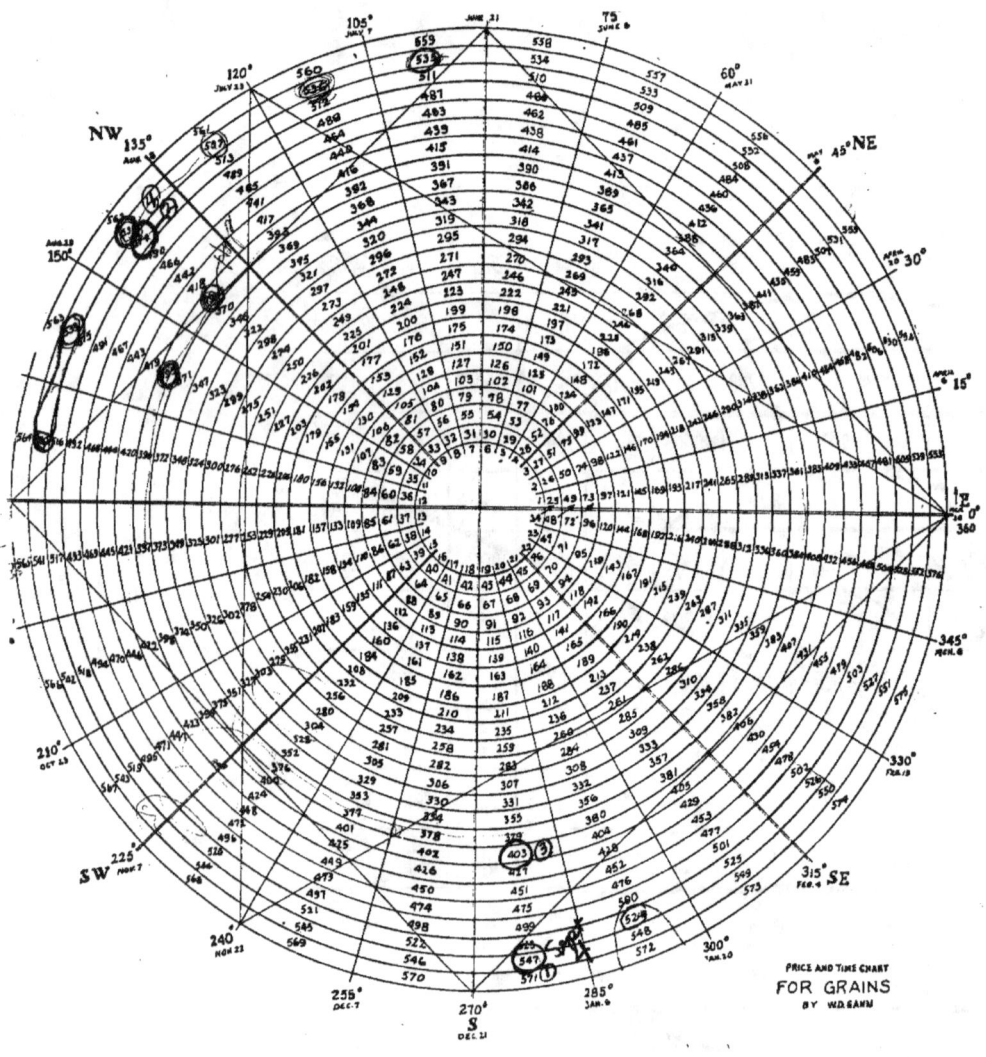

If you were to correlate the divisions of the year into this circle, it would come out as follows:

3/21
4/5
4/20
5/5
5/21
6/5
6/21
7/7
7/23
8/7
8/23
9/7
9/22
10/8
10/23
11/8
11/22
12/7
12/21
1/5
1/20
2/4
2/19
3/5

Gann said that this important chart starts with 0 and goes completely around the circle to 360 degrees. It divides the circle into 2 first and all the way down to get:
180
90
45
22 ½
11 ¼
5 5/8

It then can divide the circle by 3 and all the way down to get:
120
60,
30,
15,
7 /12

Also note that as we have said before you can place both calendar dates and degrees of the circle on the outside parameter of this chart. You can also expand this circle chart out further by using the techniques of the Excel program. It takes much time and effort to work with these charts. Continue to work with the Circle Charts beyond the examples in the book and you will be rewarded.

Gann's Hand-Drawn Circle of 72 Chart

Gann used the circle of 72 for timing points of the year. There are 72 inside numbers of 5 degrees each and 24 parameter divisions on the outside of this circle. Work with this Circle Chart as it gives you the turns of the year on many commodities and stocks.

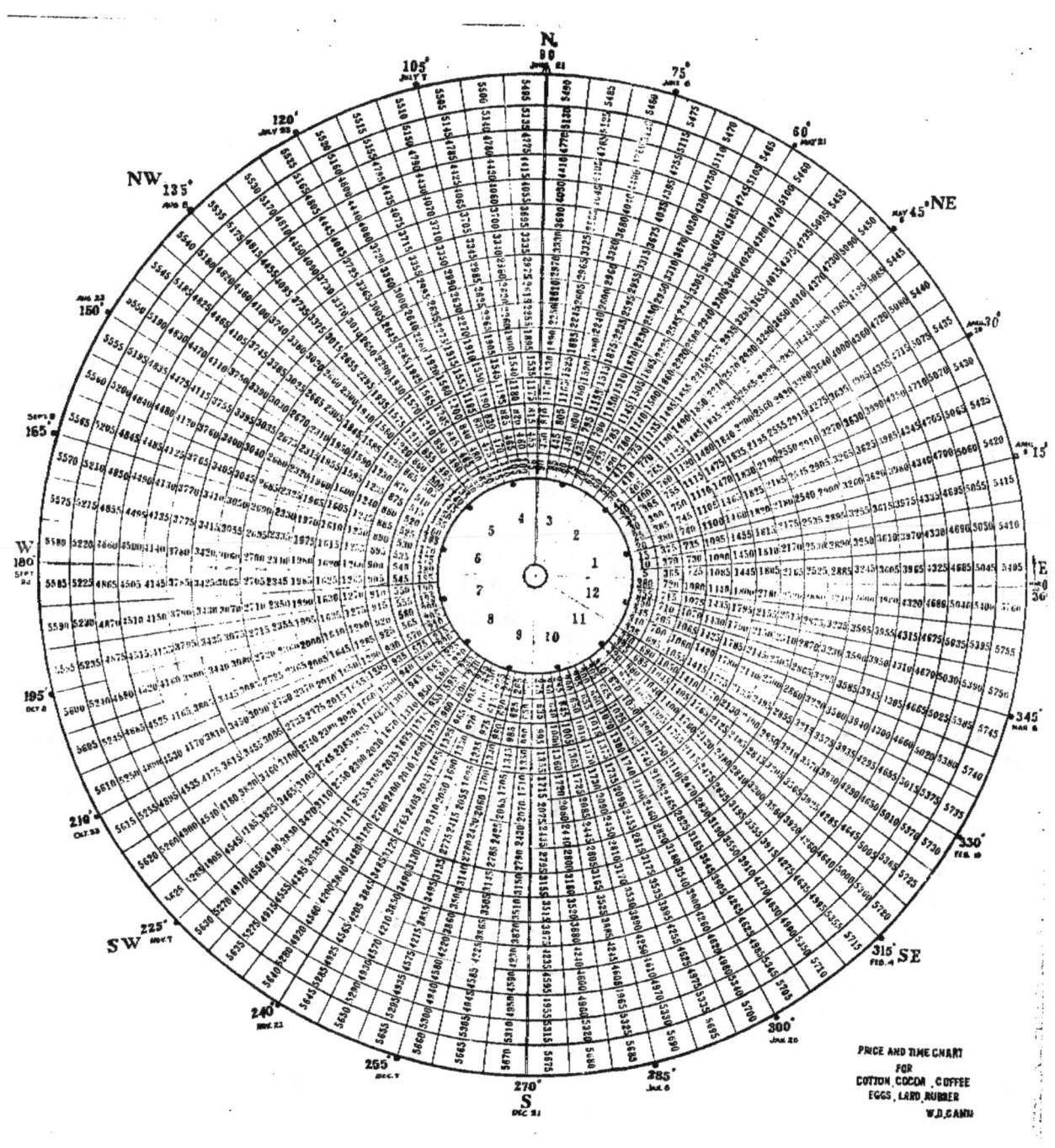

Gann's Hand-Drawn Circle of 24 Chart

The circle of divides the year into 24 equal parts. You can see on this Circle Chart that Gann labeled the outside parameter with dates of the year and degrees. You should also do that with your Excel charts. Inside prices will many times correspond with the outside parameter dates.

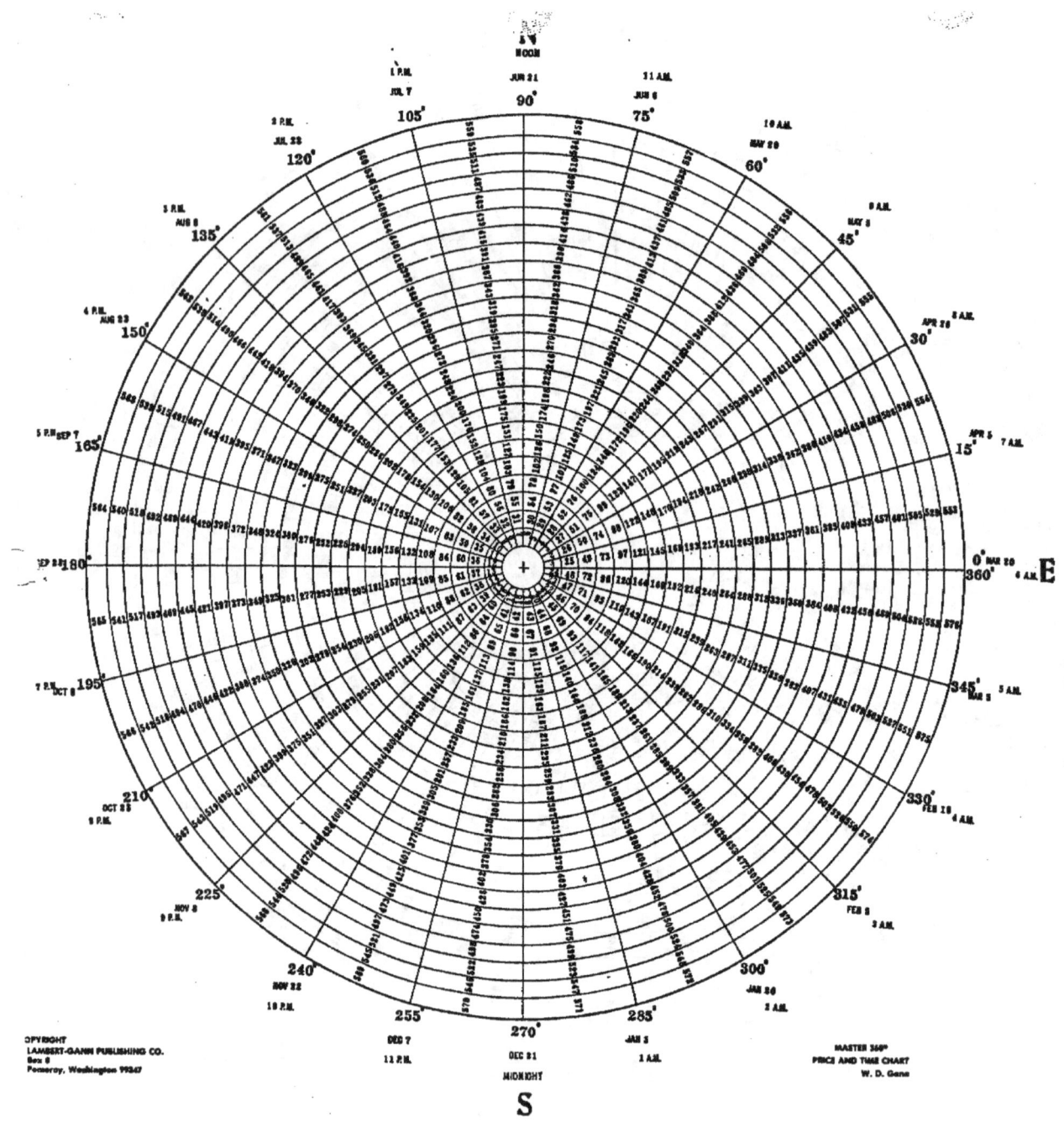

Gann's Hand-Drawn Master Time and Price Chart

This was Gann's Master Time and Price Chart, which starts out at 1 and goes around to 24 on the first circle. This is an important time chart as it corresponds with the timing of the day of 24 hours and the timing of the year of 12 months. Gann labeled this chart with 15 degrees of longitude = 15 days of time.

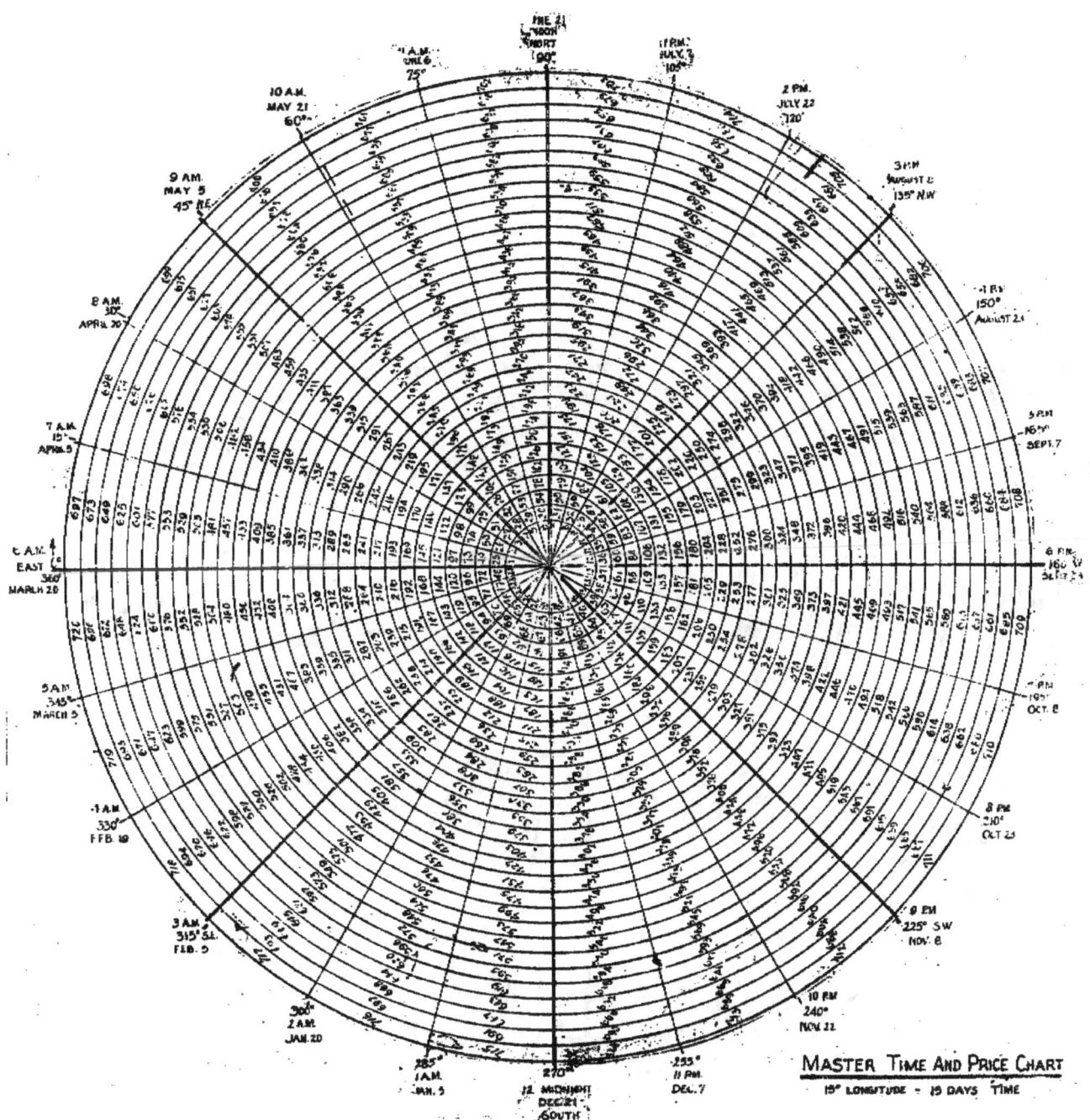

Gann's Hand-Drawn Circle Chart of 36

This is Gann's Circle Chart of 36. It's important because 36 is 1/10th of the year and the circle of 360. All-important numbers are taken from the circle and from this chart. Study it carefully.

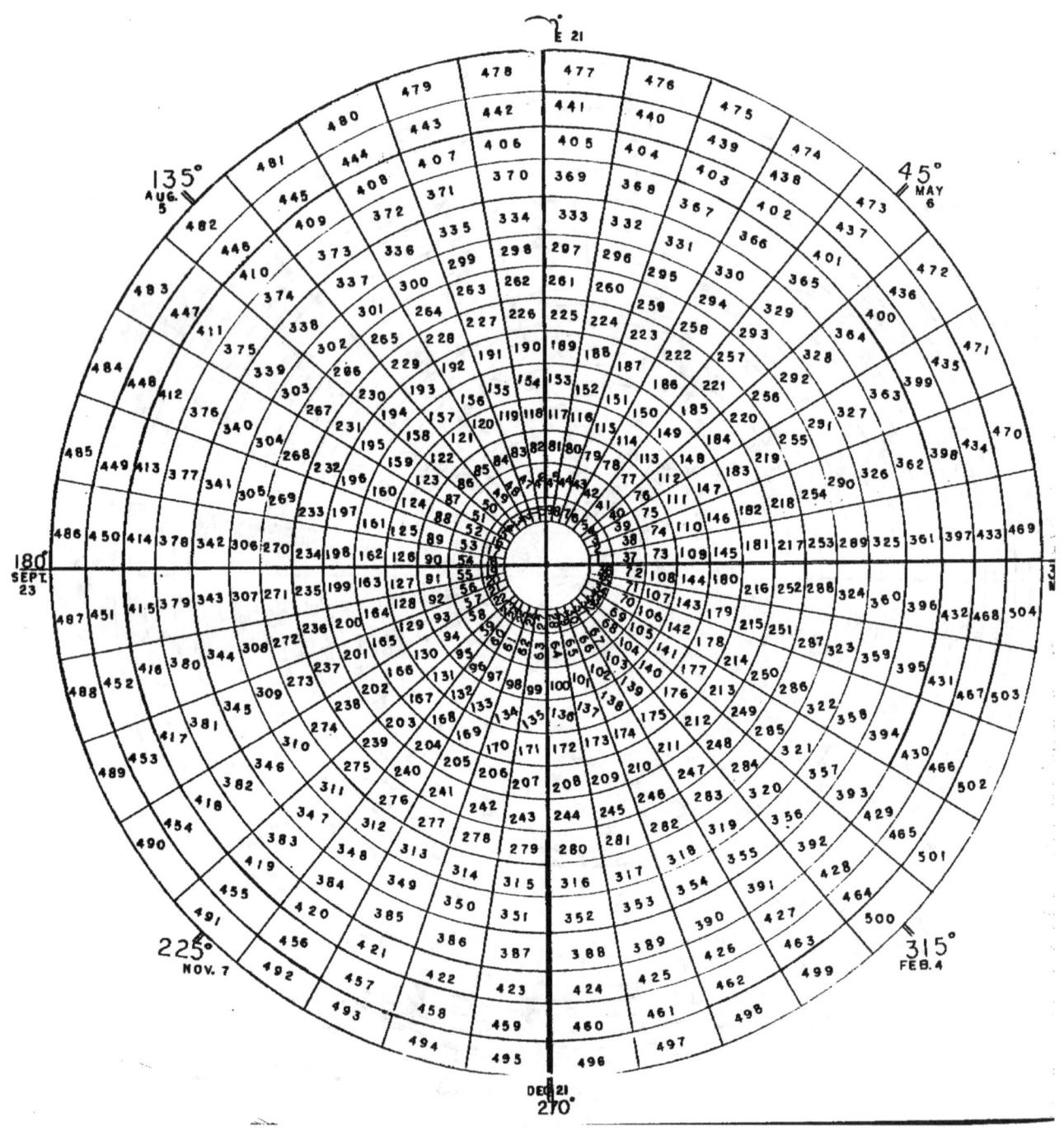

Gann's Hand-Drawn Master 360 Degree Chart

This is basically the same as Gann's Master Time and Price Chart on page 50. However, in this example, he labeled it as the Master 360 Degree Chart.

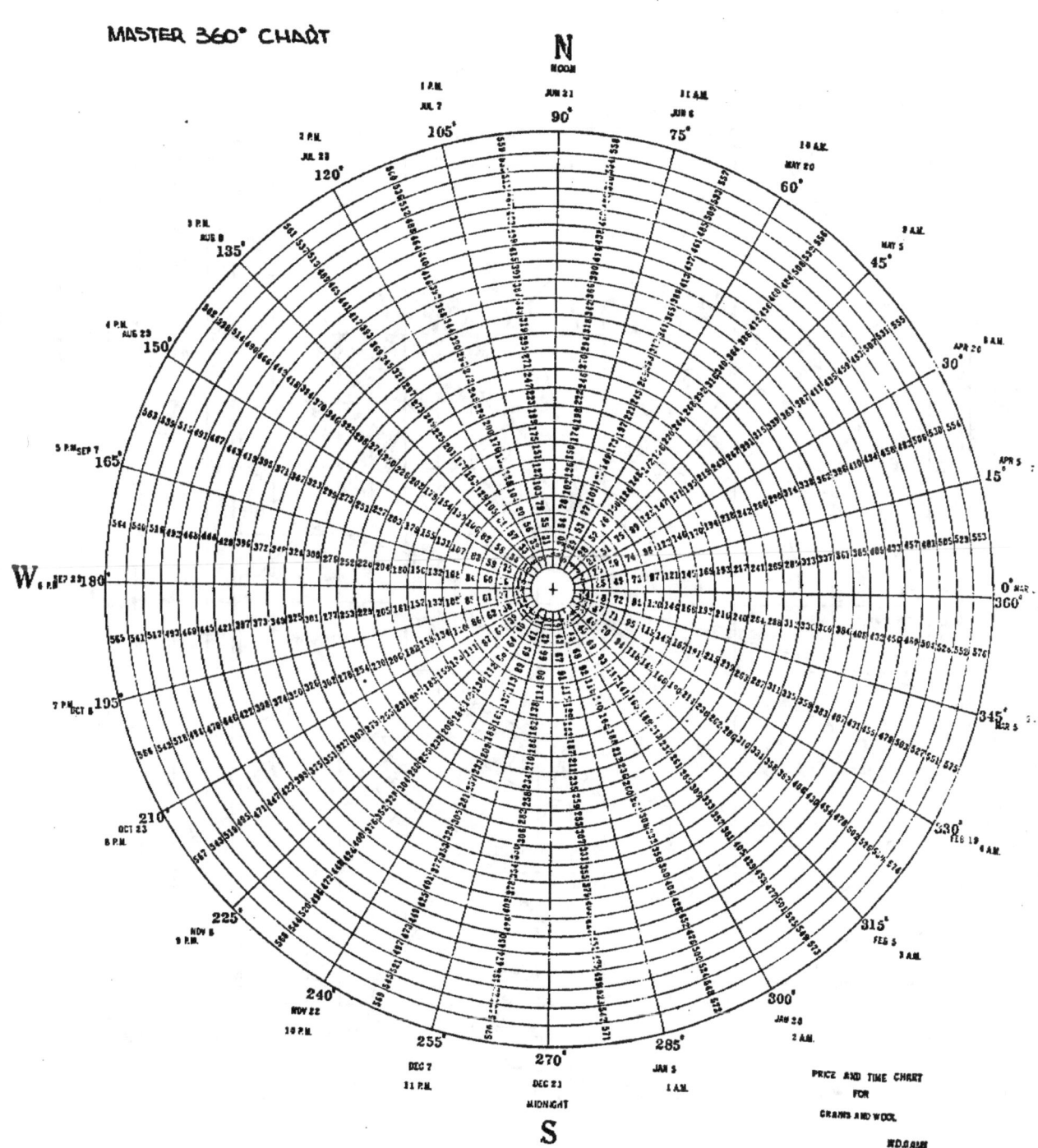

The Circle Chart and Astrology

Gann often used astrology in his trading. In this chart you can see how he marked on the chart the changes in the movements of the planets. The planets basically are the Gann angles. When a Gann angle breaks it's the same thing as a change of planetary direction. When this coincides with one of the 24 divisions of the year on a Circle Chart, you get a major change of trend in the market.

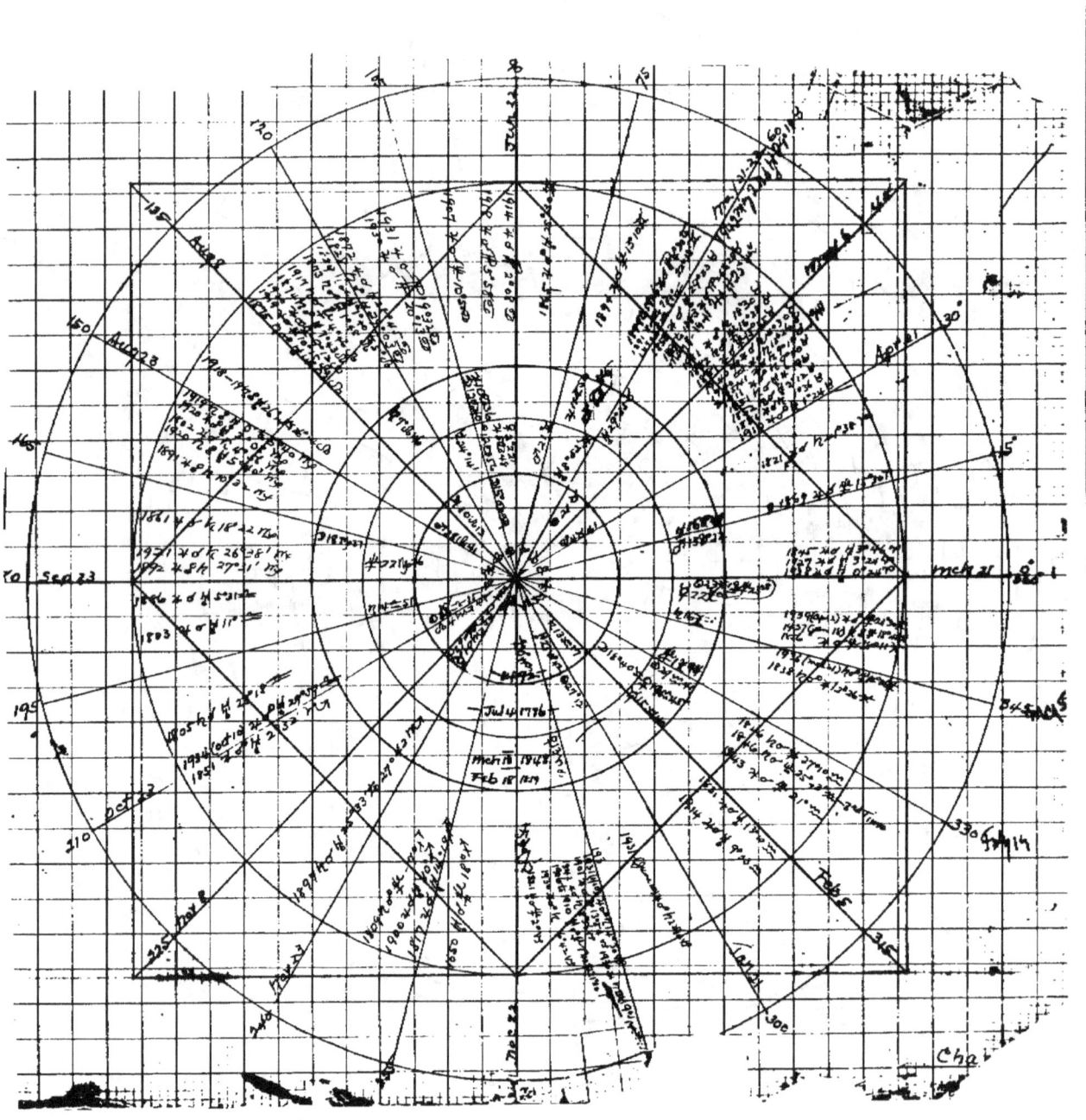

Trendlines Represent Planets

This is the famous Gann chart that everyone has in their publication to explain that Gann used astrology. Trendlines on this chart represent planets. In fact all of the natural Gann trendlines, the 1x1, the 2x1, the 3x1, etc. represent planetary movements. Usually when a planet changes direction, you will get a trendline break to the downside in an uptrend or to the upside in a downtrend. When these trendline breaks correspond to a seasonal or yearly change on the outside parameter of a square, circle, or hexagon chart, it is more important.

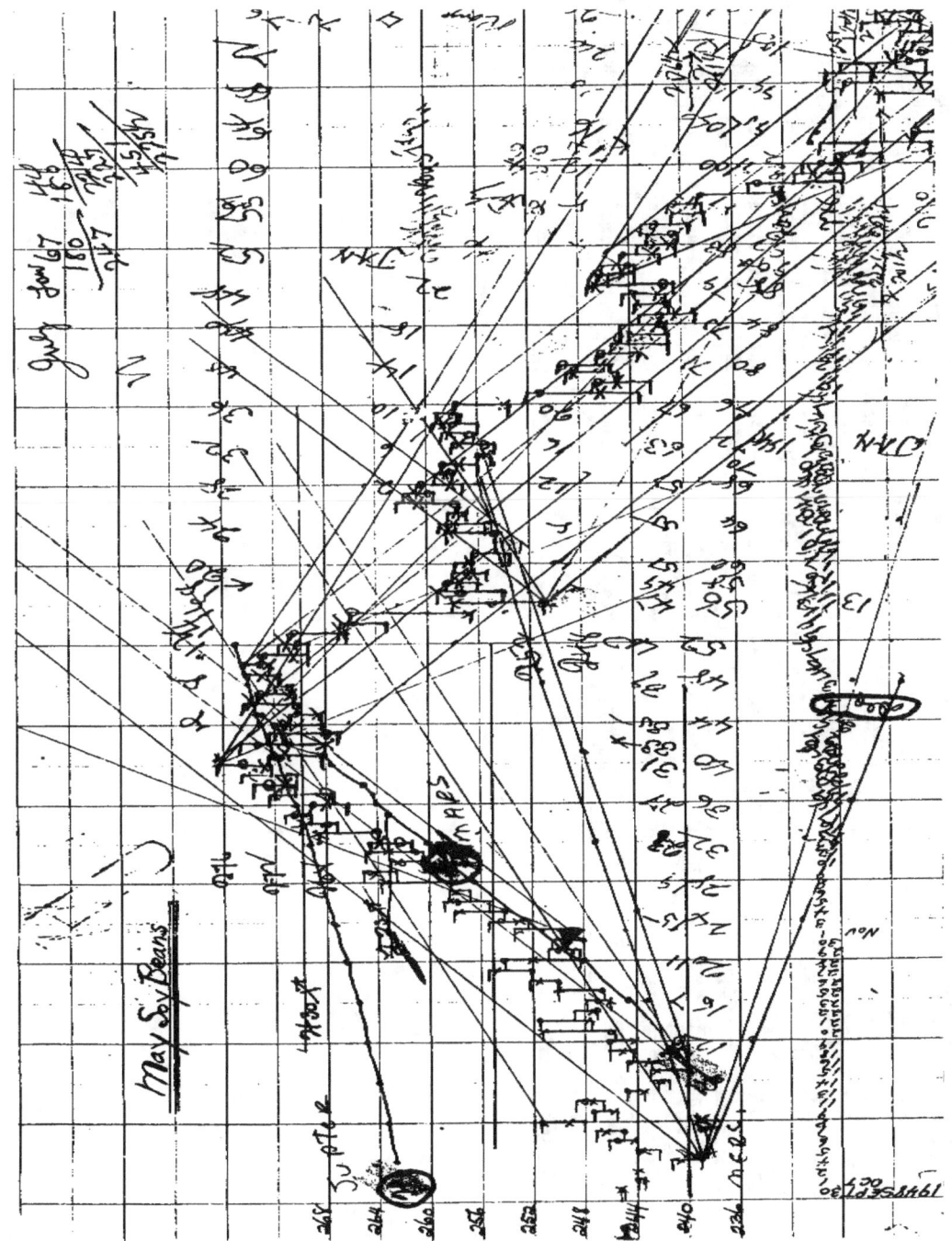

Proof of Gann's use of Astrology

You can see from Gann's personal ephemeris, that he did, in fact mark changes in the planetary movements, which corresponded to the trend changes on his trading charts.

Japanese Government Bonds Using The Circle Chart

In this example we are using the Circle Chart. Note that the low on 9/22/90 was 87. Look at the Circle Chart and note that the number closest to it is 85, which is its support. Now move up in dates until you get to 12/7/90. The number corresponding here is 90, which is way off. We should now move up 90 degrees to the next level, which, is 96. This is now the resistance.

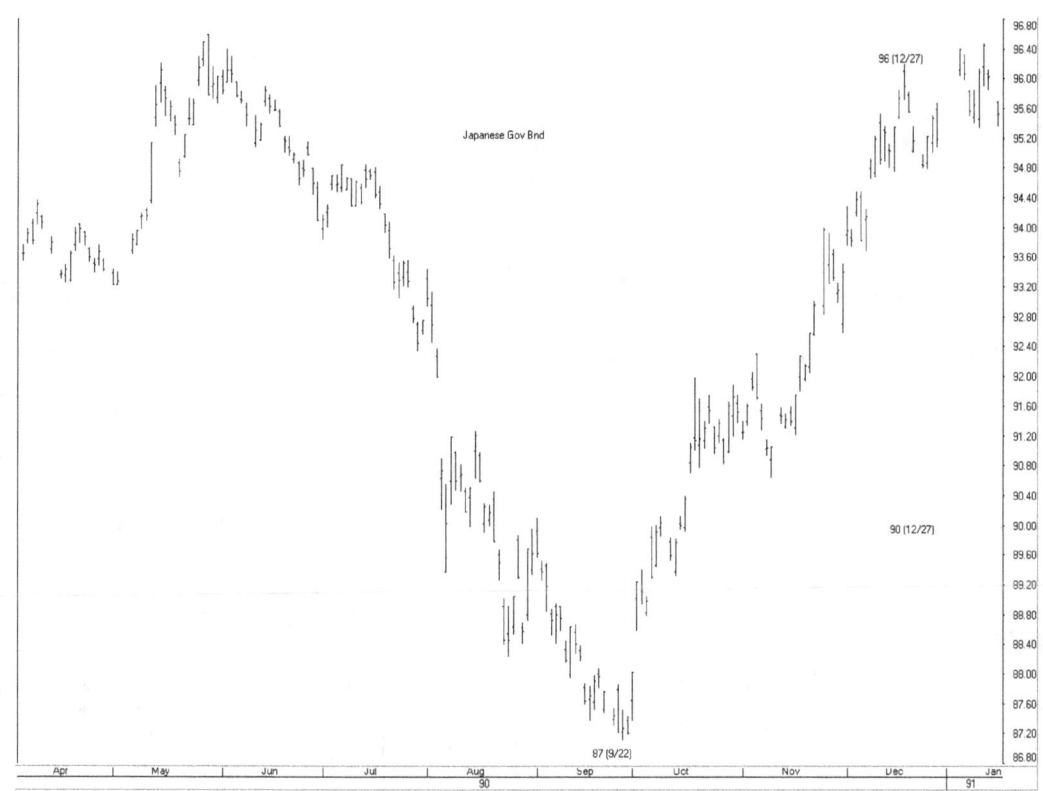

Xerox Circle Chart

On this chart we highlighted the low at 11/16/96 with a corresponding price at 16 as support. As the market moved up it made a high at 30 on 3/16/97. The support price on the circle chart is 25. Moving higher on 8/18/97 the market shows support at 35. On 10/22/97 the market topped out at 42 and the circle chart showed resistance at 62

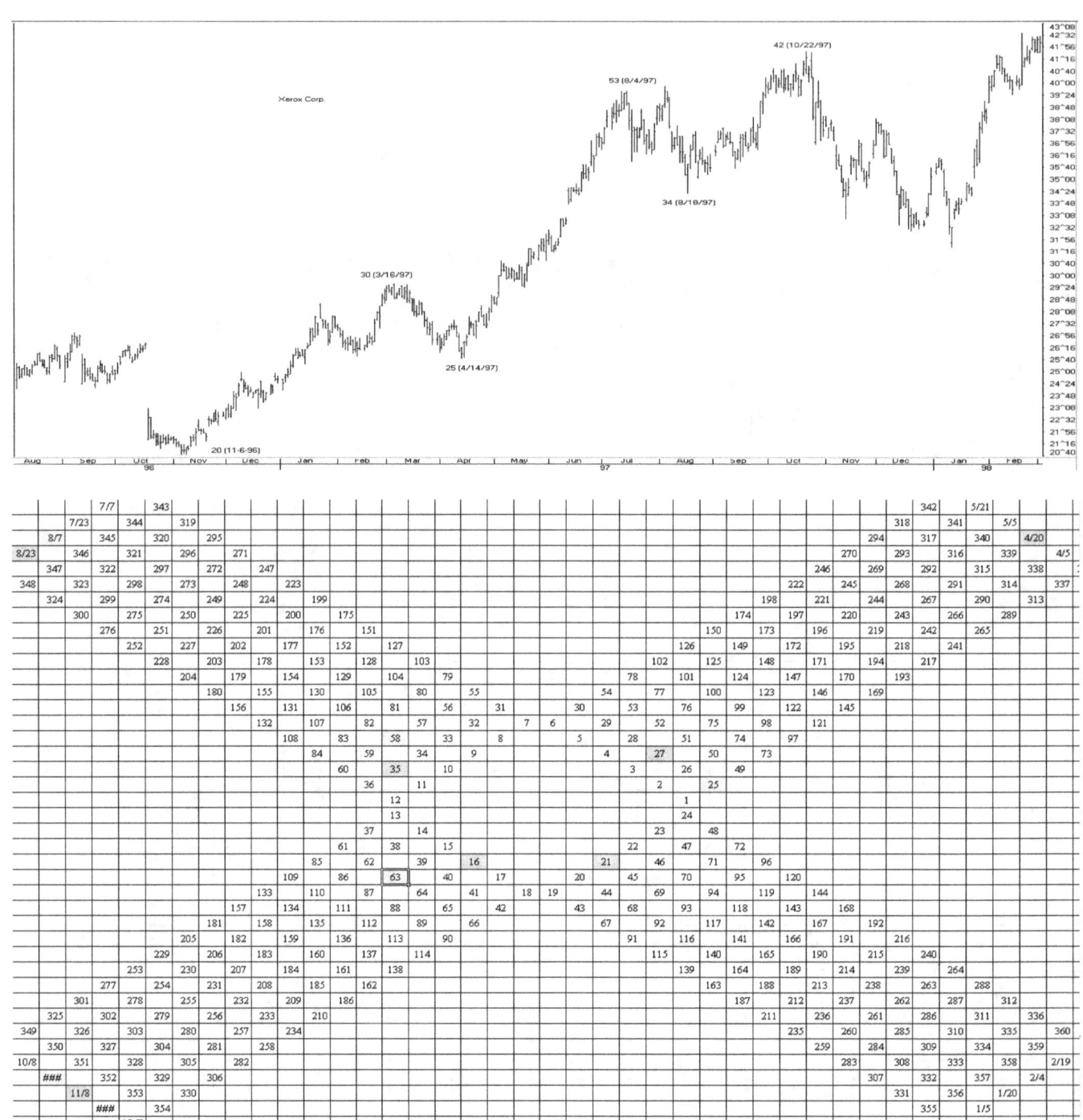

Dec Wheat Circle Chart

Using the fixed circle chart for wheat, notice it bottomed at 197 on 3/26/73. Using the circle chart on 9/7/73 the price was projected to be at 547, which it made on 9/17/73.

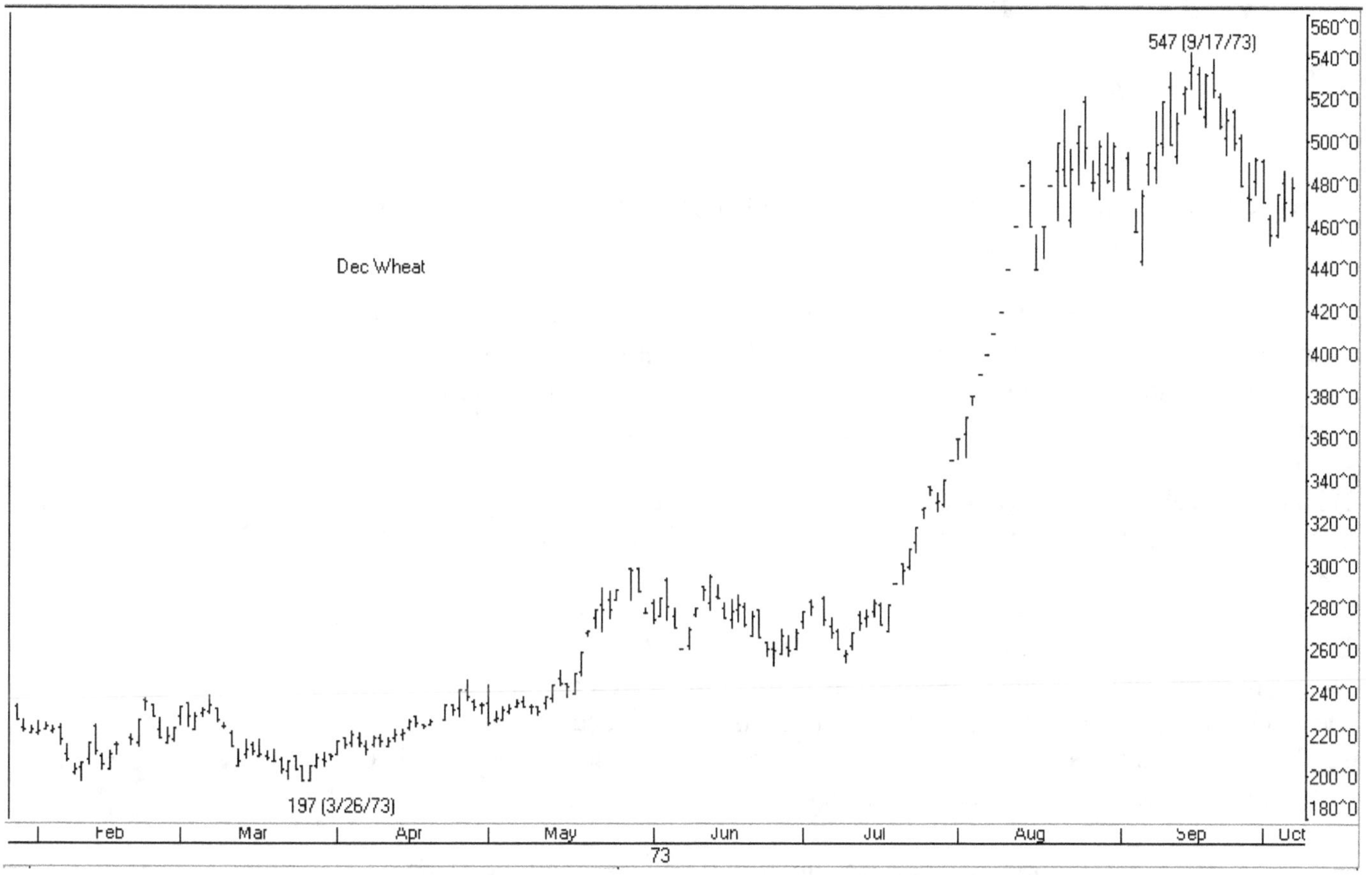

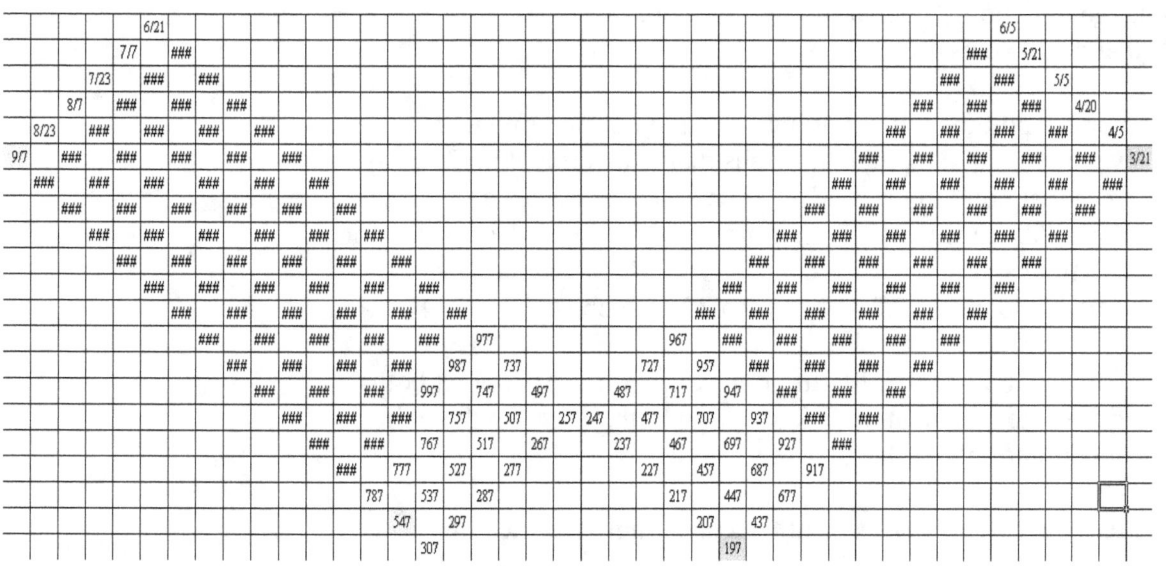

Chapter 7
Gann's Nine Math Points

Gann used nine math points for prices to stop and change direction on. Here they are and an explanation of each.

1) Resistance levels formed by natural market movements. You should scan your chart and look for visual formations or clusters of price movements. These represent resistance and support. This is where many people had previously bought and sold.

2) Natural levels of resistance and support in the Hexagon Chart and the Circle Charts. There are the vertical, horizontal and diagonal lines of resistance on these charts.

3) Gann's geometry angles, which are in fact, really planetary movement lines. These are the most important of all the nine math points given on this page. When one of Gann's angles breaks a planetary reaction is taking place. When you get a trend line break at the same time of hitting a resistance point in a square, circle or table chart, it is considered more important.

4) Timing cycles are important. When the natural timing cycles hit, the market price trend can change direction. The natural timing cycles are 5, 10, 15, 20, 30, 50, 60, 80, 90, 100 and 120 years.

5) Squaring out the price and time with previous tops and bottoms. When a market makes a low at say 2.00 on corn, that means that it will travel up 200 days, weeks, or months from that point in time. Also when a market makes a top at say 400, it will travel down 400 days, weeks or months from that top. When it does, it squares itself out with time and price. Price change is a ratio of the initial beginning price. A top at 400 might fall 400 days to 200 which is ½ of the 400.

6) The Square of Nine and the Square of Four points of resistance. Look at both of these squares and find the one the market is working with. Work up the points of resistance and support and follow them closely.

7) Highs and lows based on weekly charts and the Gann angles formed on them.

8) Highs and lows based on monthly charts and the Gann angles formed on them.

9) The Natural Cycles of Time based on the Circle of 360 degrees. The main numbers are, of course, 360, 180, 90, 45 which is the circle divided into 2's. Other important numbers are based on dividing the circle by 3, 4, 5, 6, 7, 8, and 9. Remember that the more things that hit at one point in time, the more important it is. A cluster of many resistance points can stop the market from moving forward better than just one point.

Also remember that Gann said that time is the most important factor. You should first determine if the time is up on a market and then it will be ready to change directions with price.

All of the Gann techniques can be used in combination with some of the modern day computer indicators such as stochastics, relative strength, and MACD as well as others. Keep this in mind and you can increase the effectiveness of your computer many times over.

Chapter 8
Time/Price Resistance

In the beginning man first learned to measure time by the use of the sundial. Man divided the sundial circle into 12 and then divided it again by 2 to get a division of 24. Twenty-four divisions of the circle are equal to 15 degrees in longitude. All time is basically then ruled by the sun and the 360-degree circle, which is one and the same. We therefore must assume that all time measurements in the markets are also based on the same thing, the sun and 360 degrees of the circle. The important time periods then are as follows:

Count time in days, weeks, or months from a major high or low.

Look for important changes in time based on the following time periods in days during the year. These are important divisions of the circle:

First divide the circle by 2:
$360/2 = 180$
$180/2 = 90$
$90/2 = 45$
$45/2 = 22 \frac{1}{2}$
$22 \ 1/2 \ /2 = 11 \frac{1}{4}$
(You can also divide these in half or double them to get additional numbers)

Then divide the circle by 3:
$360/3 = 120$
$120/3 = 40$
(You can also divide these in half or double them to get additional numbers)

Then divide the circle by 4:
This is the same as by 2.

Then divide the circle by 5:
$360/5 = 72$
(You can also divide these in half or double them to get additional numbers)

Then divide the circle by 6:
This is the same as by 3.

Then divide the circle by 7
$360/7 = 51.42$ = close to total number of weeks in a year

Then divide the circle by 8
This is the same as by 2 or 4.

Then divide the circle by 9
This is the same as by 3 or 6.

Early in man's existence he learned to count by the fingers on his hand and the toes on his feet. For example, 1, 2, 3, 4, 5, 6, 7 and so on…
And 5, 10, 15, 20, 25, 30, 35, 40, 45 and so on…
And 10, 20, 30, 40, 50, 60 and so on.
And 15, 30, 45, 60 and so on.
And 20, 40, 60, 80, 100 and so on.
All these numbers can be divided by half or doubled to get important harmonic extensions. These numbers are based on counting with the use of fingers or hands. These numbers can be used for both time and price calculations. See the following Sq of 100. Resistance and support points on this chart are important numbers in the markets.

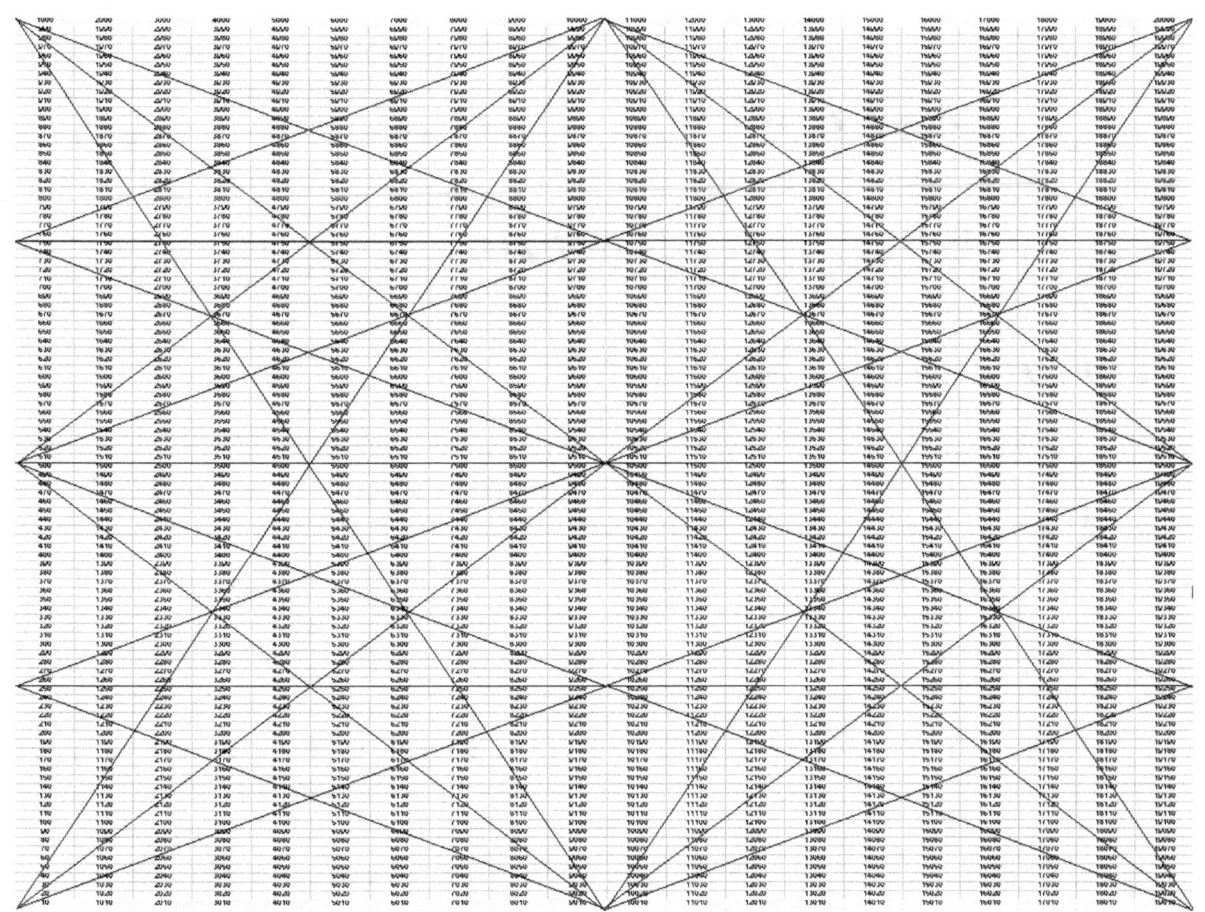

Appendix

Reprints of Square of Nine Articles

Taken from:

The Gann & Elliott Wave Magazine

Traders World Magazine

Predicting Market Trends (reprint 1.1)
Using the Square of 9

By Chris Kakasuleff

The square of nine popularized by W. D. Gann is very reliable in determining market trends. It is a useful market tool in almost all markets including stock indexes, stocks, commodities, and options. The numbers in the square of nine can be used as price levels of support and resistance, and most importantly as time units. These numbers can be used to count minutes, hours, market days, calendar days, weeks, months, and years.

First let's understand how the Square of Nine is constructed. In our illustration you see a spiral of numbers starting with one in the center, and then a commencement of numbers in a clockwise spiral that can go into infinity. In a clockwise spiral that can go into infinity. In addition overlaid on these numbers is a 360-degree circle. This circle is divided by 8, but can he divided by 16, 32, etc. When the circle is divided by 8, you have eight 45 degree angles. These angles are 0-45-90-135-I 80-225-270-315 degrees. Numbers from 2-1 1-26. etc. are on the 0 degree angle. Numbers from 3-13-31. etc. are on the 45 degree angle. Numbers 4-15-34. etc are on the 90 degree angle. Please study which numbers correspond to the balance of each 45 degree angle on the 360-degree circle.

Now that you have a fair understanding of the construction of the square of nine, lets utilize its magical powers and turn its numbers into calendar days. To begin we must decide where we're going to count calendar days. For best results, it is important to count the days from major market bottoms, or you may count the days from the birth or commencement of trading on any stock or stock index. In the stock market you could count the days from the first or commencement of trading on any stock or stock index. In the stock market you could count the days from the birth of the New York Stock Exchange on May 17th. 1972. Using this date could be tedious, hut rewarding. Another important date would be the all time modern low of the Dow Jones Industrials Average on July 8, 1932. You could experiment with the Dow low on December 6, 1974.

Probably the most useful low to count calendar days from, is the most recent major bear market low on August 12, 1982. Therefore in our example on how to utilize the square of nine, we are going to count calendar days from August 12, 1982.

First some rules and guidelines are in order here. Rule one is when the market has reached a high or low on a particular angle, then expect another high or low on the same angle in the next cycle. The next cycle is a continuation of the spiral of numbers around the circle, until they reach the same angle. As you can see in our illustration of the Square of Nine, the numbers 9, 25, 49, 81, etc all are at the end of each spiral therefore ending each cycle. An example would be if the market made a low on the 28th day in cycle 3 on the 0 degree angle of the square of nine, you would look for another low at 53 days on the 0 degree angle in cycle 4.

Another rule to follow is that market action or trends in the current cycle between the angles will generally follow the market trends that occurred in the prior cycle, between the same angles. If you have a low in the market on the 28th day in cycle 3 on the 0 degree angle and a market high on the 40th day on the 180 degree angle also in cycle 3, you can expect similar market action in cycle 4.

Rule three is the fact that at times you will be what I call psychological inversions. You will be expecting a low, as predicted on a particular angle in the last cycle, but instead on the same angle in this cycle you get a high, what you do here is invert or reverse all the highs and lows from the last cycle. If you had a low often 28 days of cycle 3 and a high at 40 days on cycle 3. but on the 0 degree angle of cycle 4 the market makes a high instead of a low then expect the market trend to be reversed. You should now expect a market low on the 180 degree angle in cycle 4, just the reverse of cycle 3 on the 180 degree angle where the market topped out. When the market reverses again, reverse the cycles back to their former pattern. In overcoming this aspect of the square of nine in trading its fairly simple to just watch the trend between the angles. IF the market action is the opposite from what it was doing in the prior cycle, the trend may be reversing. The first date we'll be calculating is April 10th, 1987, which is 1702 days from August 2, 1982. This date is on the 0 degree angle in cycle 211. To determine what may happen around April 10th, we need to refer back to the 0degree angle of cycle 20. By utilizing a hand calculator you will find that in the last cycle 1541 days is on the 0 degree angle and this corresponds to October 31, 1986. Thus 5 days later the Dow peaked at 1899 on November 5th. Therefore in this cycle we should expect another high on the same either side of 5 days. And sure enough the magic of the square of nine produces results again, as on April 6th, 1987, 4 days before 1702 days on the 0 degree angle, the Dow reached an all time high that held for more than two months.

Lets move ahead to the 45-degree angle in cycle 21. We find the number 1723, which equals May 1st 1987. In the last cycle 1561 days was on the 45-degree angle and the date was November 20th, 1986. Two days earlier the Dow bottomed on November 18th. In this cycle the market reached a low 4 days earlier on April 27, 1987, another remarkable revelation.

Before we move on to a few more examples, its important to realize that as more and more time passes from a major bean market low, the number of days between each 45-degree angle grows farther apart. Therefore its important after several months from a major low to divide the circle by 16. This gives you 16 angles between calendar days at 22 1/2 degrees apart.

This begins us at the next example. On August 25, 1987 the Dow closed at its all time high at 2722. The number of days that passed from August 12, 1982 was 1839, which is precisely on the 292 1/2 angle. On March 10th 1987 in the last cycle at 1671 days the Dow made a short team top also exactly on the 292 1/2 degree angle.

Of course there were many major factors contributing to the top on August 25th. These areas follows, August 12, 1987 marked 60 months from the low on August 12, 1982. A geometrical angle gaining 32 points per month crossed 2700 in August 1987. Also 52x52 equals 2704 the square of 52, a very important natural number. This all pointed to a major change of trend in price and time. However, I'm getting ahead of myself, as this is information for my readers in future articles.

Did the Square of Nine predict the great crash on October 19,1987. We'll as noted on April 27th the Dow reached a low 4 days early on the 45-degree angle. In the next cycle on the 45-degree angle, 1893 days equals October 18, 1987, which fell on a Sunday. The next day the Dow crashed 500 points. Of course we cannot discount the help of another major cycle at that point. As two trading days earlier on October 15th marked the end of 270 weeks, or three quarters of the cycle of 360 weeks from the low on August 12, 1982.

An interesting sideline on the Square on Nine is to realize that all angles on the cardinal squares are in harmony. That would be the 0-90-180-270 angles, and also the fixed squares 45-135-225-3 15 angles are in harmony. Let's see if this idea can produce anything of consequence. Well October 8, 1987 was 743 days from the September 25, 1985 lows. The number 743 is on the 0 degree angle. Also October 5, 1987 was 371 days from the September 29, 1986 low. The number 371 is on the 0 degree angle. October 8th, 1987 was marked 281 days from the December 31, 1986low.Thenumber281 is on the 270 degree angle. And finally October 5, 1987 marked 139 days from the May 19th low. The number 139 is on the 90 degree angle. Between October 15th and October 9th the Dow lost 158 points, the biggest losing streak in history up to that point.

One more example of our system using calendar days produced another bulls eye on November 10, 1987. This date falls one day after 1915 days which is on the 90 degree angle in the prior cycle the Dow closed at a low on May 20, 1987, two days earlier than 1744 days.

This is all hindsight now, isn't it dear reader. Therefore can the square of nine really look into the future to predict tops and bottoms? Let's put the reputation of the square of nine on the line, by predicting a market trend in the Dow after this article has gone to print. As noted earlier on August 25, 1987 the Dow reached an all time high on the 292 1/2 degree at 1939 days. In the next cycle on the 292 1/2

degree we find 2014 days have passed and the calendar date will be March 5, 1988. On this date we will expect the market to reach a high give or take a few days. Don't forget to watch out for psychological inversions. They could be dangerous to your bank account, so March 5. 1988 may turn out to be a low.
In my next article I'm going to write excerpts from an unpublished book that I'm writing about the application of the natural cycles of 45-52-144, and 360, and translating these numbers into days, weeks, and months. This article will teach you the mechanics of the division of time, and the application of the information to stock market prediction.

I'll touch on a pet theory of mine as to how these cycles are actually a time gauge for the manifestation al all events on the planet earth, thus giving us an understanding of the mechanisms of the Kharmic Wheel of Life. W. D. Gann proved the validity of this himself, by predicting in advance, World War II, the participants, when it would start, and when and how it would end, by using these very cycles.

W. D. Gann's The Tunnel Thru The Air – Reprint (1.1)

By Jim Purucker

Haven studied Gann's voluminous material since 1977, the book, which intrigued me the most was, "The Tunnel Thru The Air", written in 1927. In the forward, Gann states the book is mysterious and contains a valuable secret", clothed in veiled language. Finding this secret was an exhilarating experience. However, I could not have found it without a basic course in Astrology and the ability to use an Ephemeris.

Gann states the purpose of the book is to teach the immutable laws of nature. Immutable laws are laws which man cannot change, such as the change of seasons, weather (floods, famines), earthquakes, volcanoes and specifically the rotation of the planets and their geometrical relationships to one another. The book reveals this valuable secret by describing natural astrological cause and effect timing points, where like causes produce similar effects.

One of the greatest keys to successful trading is following these natural laws of vibration. With the secret, I was able to prove, through practical application of this timing point, Gann's Cotton trade of 1926-27, his Rye trade of 1925 and 1945, and his Coffee trade of 1954. I had found the correct beginning point to trade the minor cycle of one year. The next step involved a simple, but effective, means to square time and price from the astrological zero or beginning point. This is when I discovered the value in the square of "9". By placing an overlay over the square of "9", anchored at the center, with calendar dates on the perimeter ("a wheel within a wheel"), I could simply square price and time from any price and any date. Thus, the credit given to Gann for this innovation in naming this lifetime trading tool, "The Gann Wheel".

Because 85% of anything we learn is from what we see, I had the secret to the timing points which I could SEE WHEN they would occur in the future (Ephemeris), and the ability to SEE price and time square on the GANN WHEEL. The last step I wanted was a reliable price chart pattern, which formed at and around the vibration points to make the greatest amount of profit in the shortest period of time. Why'? Gann said. "It's much better to trade 3 or 4 times per year and make large profits, than to make 100 to 200 trades per year and be wrong half the time and finally ending up with a net loss". I finally found a reliable chart pattern which I could SEE develop at the vibration points. By using simple Gann techniques, I developed a trading plan of WHEN and HOW to enter this pattern, with a defined risk (stop). The entry in this pattern confirms the start of Gann's second section, confirms always selling the first rally or confirms buying the first break, (for ELLIOTTICIANS, confirms that start of the third wave), the biggest and best part of the price trend. The profit objective is determined by one or more squares of price on the GANN WHEEL.

LONG TRADE:
(1) Natural TIME vibration (4-13-87)'
(2) Plus 90' Square (3 months (calendar days) or (64/67 market days) (7-15-87)
(3) 59.90 Price Square, 90' (GANN WHEEL)

SHORT TRADE:
PRICE PATTERN for the greatest amount of profit in the shortest period of time. The pattern is defined by the word G-A-N-N2-S (the S is for SHORT). Enter trade by drawing 1X1 angle from N2. Enter SHORT M.O.C. on CLOSE below 1X1 angle, at 57.40 on August 5th. Place a buy stop at S (defined risk) 59.60. Next, place order to add to SHORT position by drawing a horizontal line from (A). Enter SHORT M.O.C. on CLOSE below horizontal line at 55.50 on August 14th. Next, lower stop to original enter on both positions to 57.40 (buy stop). Next, place open buy order to cover both SHORT positions at 51.00 (180' opposition from 4-13-87 on GANN WHEEL). Order filled on 8-24-87 (cancel buy stop at 57.40).

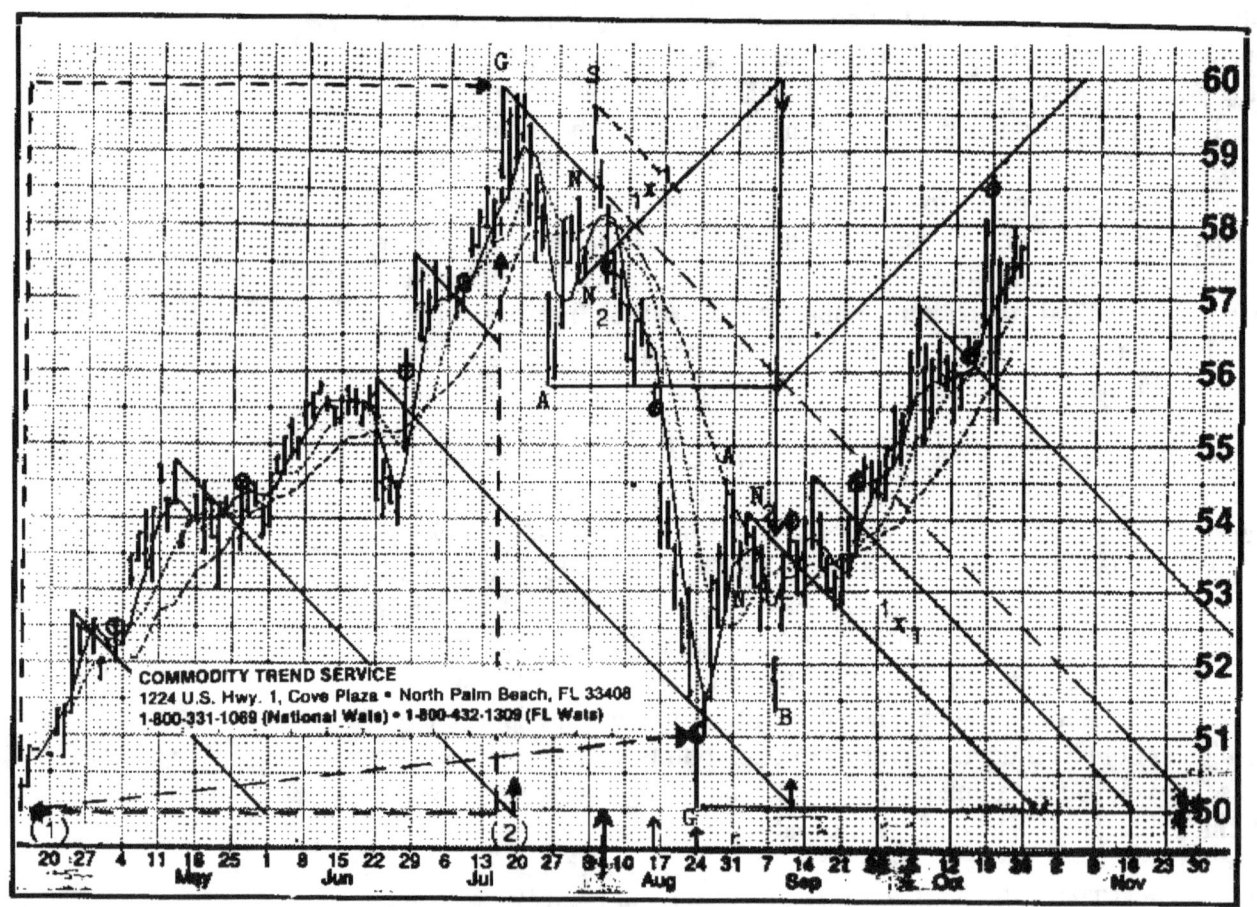

In "Sync" With Natural Laws reprint (1.2) of Cause and Effect

By Jim Purucker

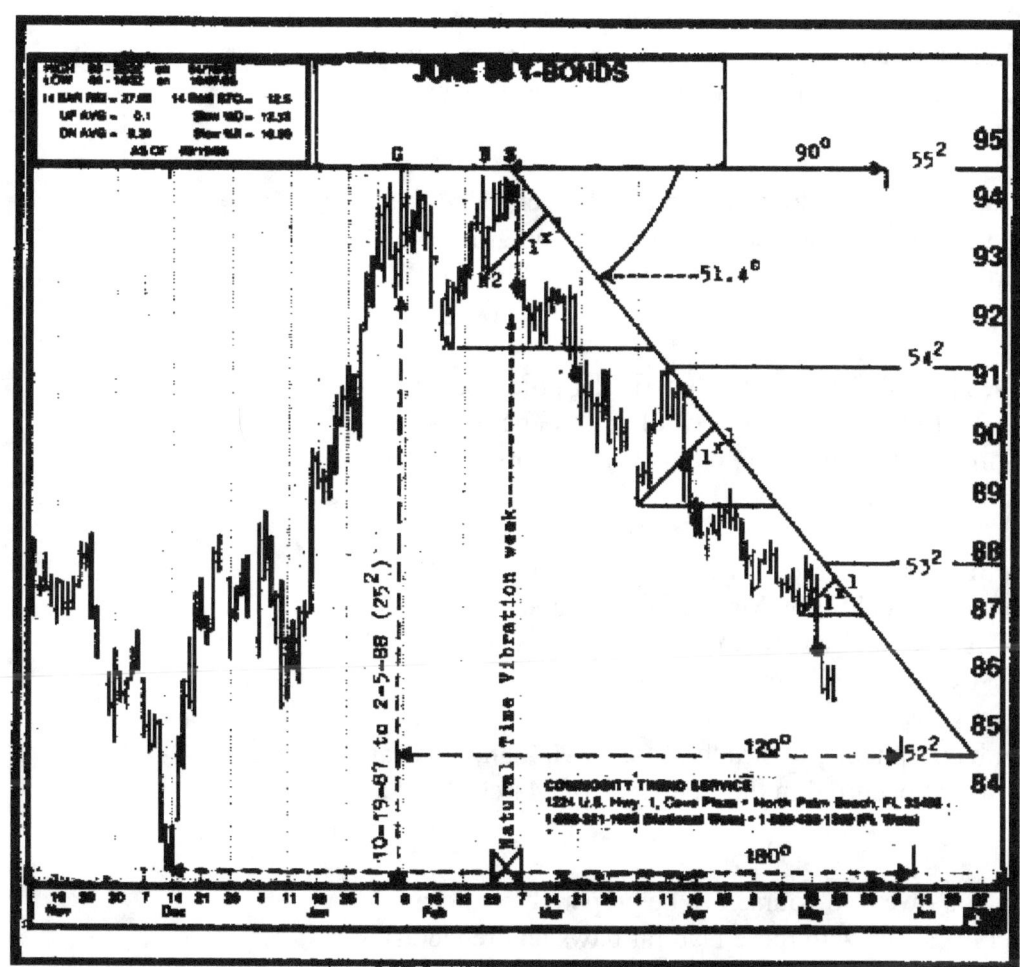

Since the February, 1988 issue of the GANN AND ELLIOT WAVE, another natural cause and effect timing point occurred the week beginning Monday, February 29 and ending Friday, March 4. Specifically, trades from the short side were presented in the T-Bonds, Muni-Bonds, T-Notes, T-Bills, and Eurodollars. Trades from the long side were presented in the Live Cattle, Hogs, Gold, Silver, Platinum, Crude Oil, Heating Oil, and CRB Index.

In chapter III of Gann's book, "How to Make Profits In Commodities," Gann states, "Time is the MOST important factor of all and not until sufficient time has expired does any big move start up or down. TIME must be allowed for accumulation (buying) or distribution (selling) BEFORE the trend can change."

Once you are aware of WHEN these natural timing points for the minor cycle of one year occur, the next step is to watch for the G-A-N-N2-(BIS) pattern to form on and around these TIME periods. Why? Because it takes TIME for accumulation or distribution to occur BEFORE the Natural Timing point is confirmed by the G-A-N-N2 price pattern. The G-A-N-N2 price pattern affords plenty of time (3-4 weeks) to SEE accumulation or distribution take place from G to B/S. As Gann says in Chapter II, page 29, of "How to Make Profits in Commodities." "When you SEE the same picture or formation occur the second and third time on and around these Natural Timing points, you KNOW what it means."

There is an old adage, "a picture is worth a thousand words." I've changed this old adage to read, "a G-A-N-N2 picture, which occurs on and around these Natural Timing points, is worth 'X' number of dollars." You can fill in the 'X' with the number of contracts you trade.

Why is the knowledge of these Natural Cause and Effect timing points so important to you as a trader? The following is an excerpt found on page 200 in Gann's book, "The Tunnel Thru the Air" which explains what occurs when these Natural Laws of Cause and Effect are violated.

Robert (Gann) was talking with an old veteran trader, Mr. Henry Watson. Mr. Watson told Robert the history of Daniel Sully. Mr. Sully had made 10 to 15 million dollars in the Cotton Market, but by violating and not following the "Natural Law." in March of 1904, he lost his whole fortune.

For those who are familiar with an Ephemeris, turn to March, 1904, and you can SEE the Natural Cause point which occurred in the first week of March, 1904, a leap year like 1988.

As an intelligent trader, don't you owe it to yourself to be prepared for these Natural Timing points and get in "sync" with these Natural Laws and reoccurring price patterns just as Gann did?

POSITION TRADE: SHORT JUNE, 1988 T-Bonds: Natural TIME vibration (2-29-88 through 3-4-88). Like produces like (3-5-87 TOP in T-Bonds).
The price pattern at the vibration point is defined by the word G-A-N-N2-S (S is for SHORT). Enter trade by drawing 1X1 angle from N2, enter SHORT M.O.C on CLOSE below 1X1 angle at 92-15 on 3-4-88. Place a buy stop at 'S' (defined risk at 94-13). Next, place an order to add to SHORT position by drawing a horizontal line from 'A'. Enter SHORT M.O.C on a CLOSE below horizontal line at 9 1-01 on 3-li-88. At this point the price, an 'M' top, has confirmed entry into Gann's second section. Next, lower buy stop to original entry to 92-15 on both positions. Next, draw a 51.4 degree angle from 55 2, 94-17 from 3-3-88, 360/7 = 51.4 degrees (51.4 degrees is the casing angle from the cardinal points to the peak on

the Great Pyramid at Gizeh).

Next, add third short position M.O.C., by drawing 1X1 angle from 4-4-88 (after price touched 54 2 9 1-04, Even Square Pyramid Block on the GANN WHEEL square of '9') on close below 1X1 angle at 89-16 on 4-14-88. Next, draw horizontal line from 4-4-8 8 low and add fourth short position M.O.C. on close below horizontal line at 88-18 on 4-18-88. Next, lower buy stop to 89-16 on four short positions. Next, add fifth short position by drawing 1X1 angle from 5-12-88 at 86-29 and horizontal line from 5-12-88 (after price touched 53 2, 87-25, odd square Pyramid Block). Short M.O.C. on 5-17-88 at 86-10. Next, lower buy stop to 87-26 on five short positions. Next, as we are coming into the contract month, June as this is being written, place an order to cover the five short positions at 84-13 (18 2), otherwise, cover at the close on 5-31-88 and switch to September, 1988 TBonds.

In Gann's book, pages 43-44, "How to Profit From Commodities." Gann lists 28 Valuable Rules and states, "Anyone who follows them will make a success." The Key word is FOLLOW. Throughout the June TBond trade, Rule #25 was FOLLOWED. Rule #25 states, "Don't guess what the trend is. Let the market PROVE what the trend is."

Gann and the Circle reprint (1.3)

By Chris Kakasuleff

In order to pin point the manifestation of events upon the physical earth plane, you must first have a working knowledge of the astronomical mathematical formula. The 360-degree cycle popularized by W. D. Gann is our reference point. What did the wizard of Wall Street teach us about the great 360-degree cycle? The mathematical architect Gann generously left us a legacy of cosmic information to formulate into working principles to predict in advance short, intermediate, and long-term financial market trends.

In my long cerebral journeys into the very core of the secrets of the universe, time and time again nature has unveiled its self-tome by proving that its greatest secrets are revealed in an essence of simplicity.

Mr. Gann articulated that the jewel of the 360-degree cycle in predicting stock market trends was literally calendar time. Let's make sure I heard myself correctly here. I said that to beat mighty Wall Street all I needed as working tools was a calendar and maybe a calculator. What a powerful tool this concept is. Let's now construct a foundation and manifest working principles for this earth shattering news.

To become the captain of our destiny in profitable stock transactions we need to follow certain guidelines and rules. First we must transpose calendar time onto the 360-degree circle. To devise our formula we must gaze upon the heavens and monitor the cosmic clock that regulates the motion of mother earth. The earth completes one revolution around the sun in 365.24 days.

To reconcile our revelation of calendar time being the domain for predicting market trends, we simply recognize the fact that the earth itself is at the mercy of the gravitational pull of the sun, therefore dictating its annual cycle of 365.24 days. As the Earth and its consciousness is the subordinate of the sun, so man and the manifestation of all events on earth are in harmony with this same cosmic music of 365.24. Can you believe the simplicity of natures most guarded secrets? Mr. Gann taught us that the beginning of each renewed annual Earth cycle commenced at the spring equinox. Gann indicated that by counting days from March 21 that many of nature's invisible secrets would be revealed. Gann went on to say that by no means was the stock market devoid or divorced from this natural calendar rhythm.

Just as the Earth has seasons of the year; a time to plant, a time to cultivate, a time to grow, a time to pluck, and a time to reap, so does Wall Street ebb and flow with this same circadian time piece.

My dear friend, please take time now to grasp this essence of universal law. Understand and cherish it as your eleventh commandment. By programming it into your belief system and consciously recognizing its manifestations in the drama of your own life's enfoldment, you will then posses in your heart a glimpse of the truth of all things. You will understand that life deals out no random events. You will cherish the fact that you indeed are the navigator of your life's destiny. You will discover the more you scratch at truth, the more it will itch.

As I mentioned earlier, Gann taught us that one avenue of endeavor using the cycle 365.24 was to mark time from March 21. 1-Ic said to start by making March 21 our zero point. Thus making March 22 day one. Gann divided the year into six teen equal parts. By dividing the year by four, our sum is the beginning of each new season of the year.

The philosophy Gann was spot-lighting onto our tunnel vision was that March 21 was the commencement of the annual reincarnation of life's new birth. By June 21 at the summer solstice point. Intense new growth had taken place in the animal, vegetable, plant, and insect kingdom. By the fall equinox on September 21 the peak of vitality was ebbing ever so slowly, and old age was replacing fruitarian as the dominant cycle. By the winter solstice, frozen and suspended animation ruled the northern hemisphere of the earth, and the suspended seeds of the perpetuation of life were invisible, as all life was hidden in the frozen tundra, meditating patiently for the return of the photons of light in the spring.

The wizard then instructed us to divide the year by eight. This gives us four more dates to consider. These are the halfway points of spring, summer, fall, and winter. Gann said to also divide the year by sixteen. This finally gives us sixteen important calendar days as our focus.

Gann told us that the most powerful resonating points using calendar time was six months or 180 degrees from the beginning point and then back around to the anniversary date itself. As summer becomes very hot and winter reaches frigid temperature extremes 182 days later, so too does stock market action reach volatile extremes. What goes around truly does come back around.

The next important model points are the one quarter points. Using our calendar we quickly realize that these points are 91 days apart. Gann said to expect a change of trend in the stock market at these points. Our analogy concerning confirms this rule, as each season of the year guarantees a change of trend in climate conditions.

Gann went on to suggest that by dividing the year by eight, into 45 day increments, we would find more wheels within wheels. The changing gears of market trends can easily become visible on any bar chart for those who recognize the signposts of calendar time.

Gann finally encouraged us to divide the calendar year by 16. This gives us a complete road map and blue print to predict in advance changes of trend in stock market forecasting.

Here is a listing of Gann's natural calendar year cycle. Each of these dates are approximately 22 and one-half days apart. Gann tells us to expect general changes of trend year in and year out, based on these natural time frames.

Anyone who is curious enough to research these dates will have discovered a new book of revelations. By just scooping the first two dates on our chart for the Dow Jones Industrial Average for 1988 should be an eye opener. The Dow closed at its first high for 1988 on Friday, March 18 at 2087. This date is one trading day before March 21. On our second date of April 12, which corresponds to the 22 and one-half degree angle of the circle, the Dow closed at post crash highs at 2110 exactly on April 12. Two trading days later the Dow water-falled 100 points in one day, confirming a change of trend.

This particular method of marking calendar time from March 21 is more appropriate for commodities, and raw materials that depend on the cycles of the seasons of the earth year.

An interesting sideline would be to take a closer look at the number 365.24. By multiplying this number by seven our sum total is 2556.68 days. This turns out to be precisely seven years of course, and the notorious seven year itch. The remarkable mind-boggler here is that 2556.68 days equals out to exactly 365.24 weeks. This new information totally vindicates the perfect time cycle as being 365.24 and not 360. Anyone who has the capacity to computer generate the complete cycles of 365.24 days, weeks, or years will find the mathematical validity of this sun generated number in stock market tops and bottoms. W. D. Gann discussed many times the power of the number seven in stock market action.

The timing of this article could prove to be quite revealing as August 12, 1989 is 2556.68 days or 365.24 weeks from August 12. 1982. The aging bull will be seven years old on that day.

Remember micro-man/woman is trapped unconsciously in this same fly paper cycle. All events upon the earth whether generated by group consciousness or individual karmic patterns must flow with the movement of these cosmic energies of space and time.

In my last article I discussed the power of the square of nine in predicting short term market highs and lows. We utilized this system to predict a short term high on March 5, 1988.

Well, it looks like we've got bragging rights, as the Dow Jones Industrial Average closed at 2081 on Tuesday, March 8, only two trading days from March 5, which fell on a Saturday. This short term top was the post crash high up to that point, with a second top one trading day before the spring equinox on March 18, a Friday.

Is there a way to utilize this cycle of 365.24 to trade the market? There are specific rules to follow that I have found over time to be extremely dependable in trading stocks, stock options and stock index options. But, I don't want to give away all my secrets.

Gann's Pyramid And Fourth Factor Volume reprint (1.3)

By Jim Purucker

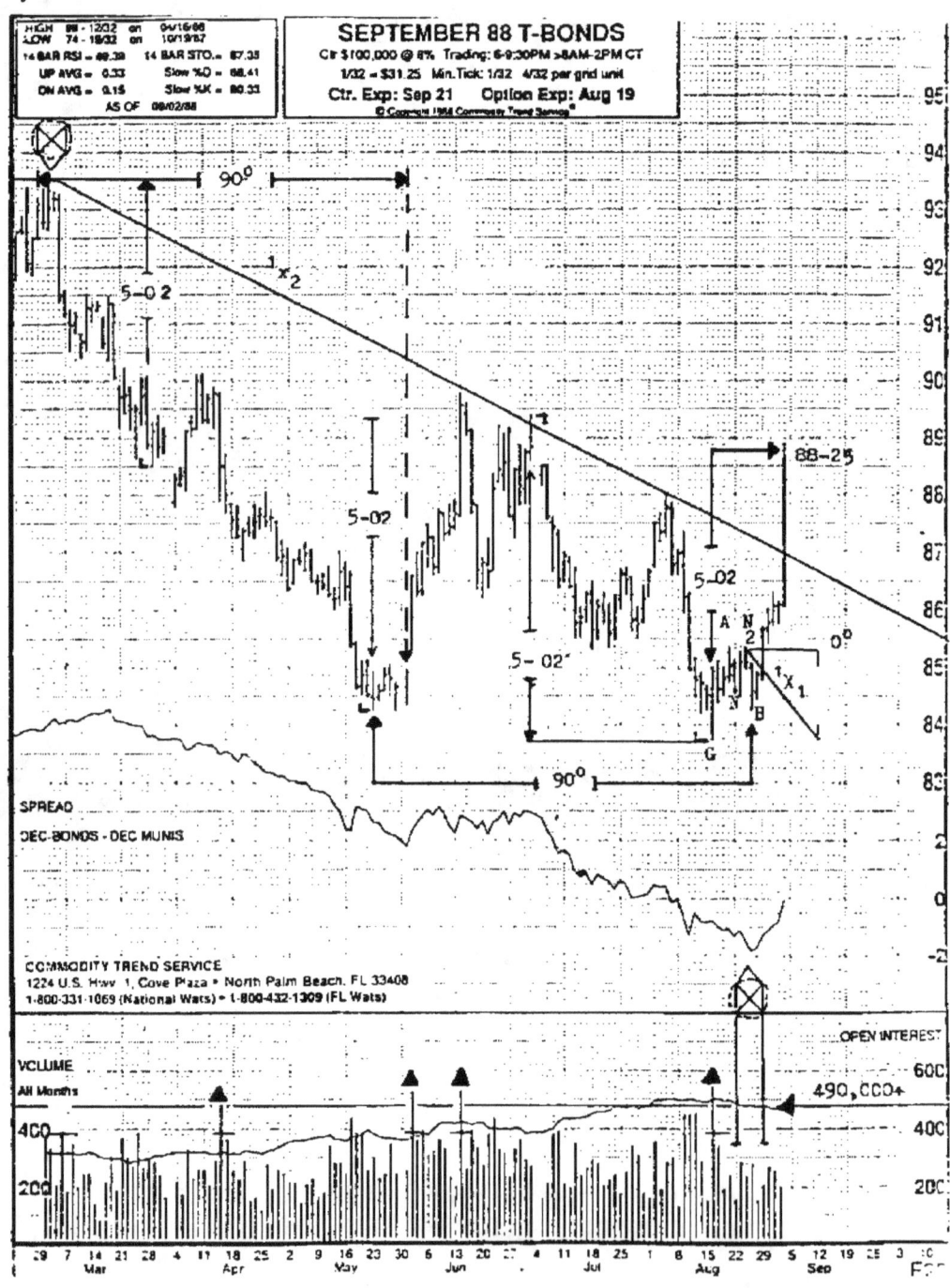

On page 62 of Gann's book, How To Make Profits in Commodities, Gann states, 'After considering three important factors, time, formations, and resistance levels, the fourth and next very important factor is volume of sales. The volume of sales is the real driving power behind the market and shows whether supply and demand are increasing or decreasing. Large buying and selling orders are shown in the volume of sales. Therefore, a careful study of the volume of sales will assist in determining a change in trend, ESPECIALLY AFTER APPLYING THE OTHER THREE FACTORS OF TIME, FORMATION AND RESISTANCE LEVELS."

In the previous articles of the Gann & Elliott Wave the first three factors were presented for illustration. First, the astrological TIMING points for trading the minor cycle of one year. Second, the G-A-N-N2-B/S (buy/sell) FORMATION, what it is and how to define it, and when to act upon proven confirmation of the pattern following Rule number 25, implementing an OFF-CON (I) & (2) condition. The third factor of importance was determining from a zero-degree beginning point of TIME, a square (90 degrees) or trine (120 degrees) in time or price on the GANN WHEEL, combined with the odd and even natural square-root numbers on the GANN WHEEL for support-resistance levels. The odd squares begin at the peak of the Gann Wheel, the Great Pyramid of Gizeh, with number one as the capstone. The next square root level, square or course of stones, begin at number two and ends with number nine or Y (three squared). The square root of these odd numbers, which fall on the fixed angle of 41.475232 degrees to the South-West compass point, are the cornerstones for each course or square on the Great Pyramid.

An example in the previous article for the price high (2-5-88) on June '88 TBonds was 94-17. Converting 94-17 to 1/32nd Bond ticks (94 x 32 + 17) equals 3025 ticks. The square root of 30252 equals 55 (55 x 55), an important resistance level. On the GANN WHEEL, the zero-degree line intersecting the two-digit number 75 (10-19-87) price low is 180 degree opposition number 94, or 19 bond points. The difference in ticks was 625 ticks (25Th 625 divided by 32nds equals 19-17 bond points. Therefore, number 75 (75-00) plus 19-17, equals 2-5-88 PRICE HIGH at 94-17 (TO THE TICK)!

Now let's analyze the September '88 T-Bonds. First, the astrological TIMING POINT to balance the week of 2-29-88 (l80) is due the week of 8-22-88, 9(1 square the week of 5-23-88 is 8-22-88. Price was 90~ square from 93-17 to 83-17, within nine ticks of the low price of 83-23 on the GANN WHEEL. Second, the G-A-N-N2- Buy formation began zero degrees on 8-16-88, marked "G" at 83-23, "A" formed at 85-11 on 8-19-88, on 8-23-88, "N", signaling a PREPARE TO BUY condition (OFF-CON 2).

At this point, a brief description of an OFF-CON condition I & 2 (OFE)nsive (CON)dition is in order. In the movie, "WAR GAMES" DEE-CON (DEF-ensive CON-ditions) were progressive stages of readiness prior to missile launch.

For brevity, I only use two conditions of readiness rather than the four conditions in the movie. A stage (2) OFF-CON is "PREPARE TO BUY," a stage (I) OFF-CON is the actual pulling the trigger for the buy executions CONFIRMING the

G-A-N-N2-Buy formation, similar to the DEFCON (I) condition in the movie, where the missiles are actually launched.

Now, let's pick up on 8-25-88 when the price drops below 84-16, the price low of "N", which signals an OFF-CON (2) state of readiness, PREPARE TO BUY condition. OFF-CON (2) also gives the right to draw a I x I angle from N2 where the buy stop orders are placed. The I x I angle from N2 was at 84-31 on 8-2-88. For those traders who have substantial amounts of capital to risk

(Fund Managers, Banks, S&Ls, Insurance Companies. Corporations and high-net-worth individuals), I suggest a TOTAL PYRAMID contract position of 10, 100, 1,000, 10,000, or 100,000 or more, using a 5-3-2=10, or 500-300-200=1,000 sequence to build the pyramid properly.

For this hypothetical trade, 1,000 contracts are placed thus: Place a Buy Stop for 500 contracts five bond ticks above the I x I angle of (84-31) at 85-04, next place a buy stop for 300 contracts one bond tick above "A" (85-Il) the zero degree horizontal at 85-12, add the final 200 contracts M.O.C. at 85-21, as long as the CLOSE is above the I x I angle from N2 and in the top 1/3 of the total price range for a total pyramid of I,000 contract. The initial sell stop is one tick below the low of the day the price closes above the I x I angle at 84-24. Initial risk is 18 bond ticks or $563.5() per contract (x) 1,000 TOTAL PYRAMID, or $562,500. plus commissions, fees and of course, any slippage for poor fills.

August 29, 1988 was a unique trading day in the OFF-CON (I) BUY execution, as the TOTAL Pyramid of 1.000 contracts were triggered and secured by the close of the 29th. On 8-29-88, the G-A-N-N2-Buy formation confirmed OFF-CON (I) condition with entry into Gann's second section.

The first objective to sell is 162 bond ticks added to the 83-23 low at "G". One-hundred and sixty two bond ticks divided by 32 equals 5-02 bond points (83-23 + 5-02) 88-25 objective. Previous vibrations of 5-02 bond points (1+6+2=9). Why nine'? The number nine seems to have a definite "power" or "vibration."

Pythagoras is believed to have had a remarkable "WHEEL" by means of which he could predict future events. Look at the design and construction of the GANN WHEEL (see ad in the GANN & ELLIOTT WAVE) the Trines 120Th240=9, l44=1+4+4=9, 216=2+1+6=9, 288=2±8+8=l8, or 1+8=9, 72=7±2=9 and 360=3+6+0=9. Gann's MASTER NUMBER 45=I+2+3+4+5+6+7+8±9454+59 Nine is the basis of the unit value of ALL numbers. On Friday, 9-2-88, the price objective 88-25 was executed. Average cost for 1,000 contracts was 85-10. 88-25 minus 85-10 equals 3-15 Bond Points, or $3,468.75 per contract times 1,000 equals $3,468,750, less commissions, fees, and slippage.

Now, Gann's fourth factor VOLUME OF SALES as another KEY, significant in trading T-Bonds. Notice the KEY TO DAILY VOLUME at trend turning points is 490,000+ contracts on 4-14-88, 6-1-88, 6-14-88, and 8-16-88. Here Gann says the trade has made up its mind, a change of trend is eminent and reveals it through ONE-DAY VOLUME of 490,000+ contracts. Yet, even with the KEY TO VOLUME, Gann, in his infinite wisdom, says, "In order to be a success, "FOLLOW A DEFINITE RULE." Remember Gann's rule number 25? Let the market prove ills at bottom with the G-A-NN2-B formation as the formation, provided nine trading days of accumulation prior to confirmation of entry in OFF-CON (I) on 8-29-88.

In conclusion, I would like to make you aware of two Aphorisms of Pythagoras, number four and number nine (an aphorism is a short pointed sentence expressing a wise, clever observation or general truth). Number four states, "assist a man in raising or lifting his burden; but, do not assist him in laying it down."

In this article I have done my best to help and assist you in your trading by giving you the tools to raise yourself up and out of the 90 percent losers, 10 percent winners ratio, which because of human nature, stays the same every year. However, you must be responsible for your losses, as well as your gains, and not place the blame for your losses on others.

Pythagoras' aphorism number nine states, "offer not your right hand easily to anyone." This statement warns not to offer wisdom and knowledge to those who are incapable of appreciating them. Gann would cast a birth chart (horoscope) of the individual purchasing his courses. In this way, he was trying to determine if the individual was skeptical or was capable of studying long and hard about the truths he was trying to teach. Gann wrote voluminous am-mounts of material to create a desire in the individual to search for hidden truths, much in the same way the ancients in the past clothed their secrets in veiled language; such as the writers of the Bible, Plato, Aristotle, and Pythagoras, to name a few.

Gann, in his wisdom, realized the unregenerate do not desire wisdom and knowledge, but through indolence would eventually cut off the right hand that was extended in kindness to them. Once one learns to like themselves, has a continuous positive winning attitude, takes responsibility, practices the greatest of virtues-patience, and follows a disciplined technical approach to Gann's rules, then, and only then, will it be your time and season to reap material wealth. Many of my clients who have purchased the GANN WHEEL are extremely successful men and women in many different fields of endeavor. These people know how to get the job done

How to Make the Greatest Profit reprint (1.4)

By Jim Purucker and Pat Reda

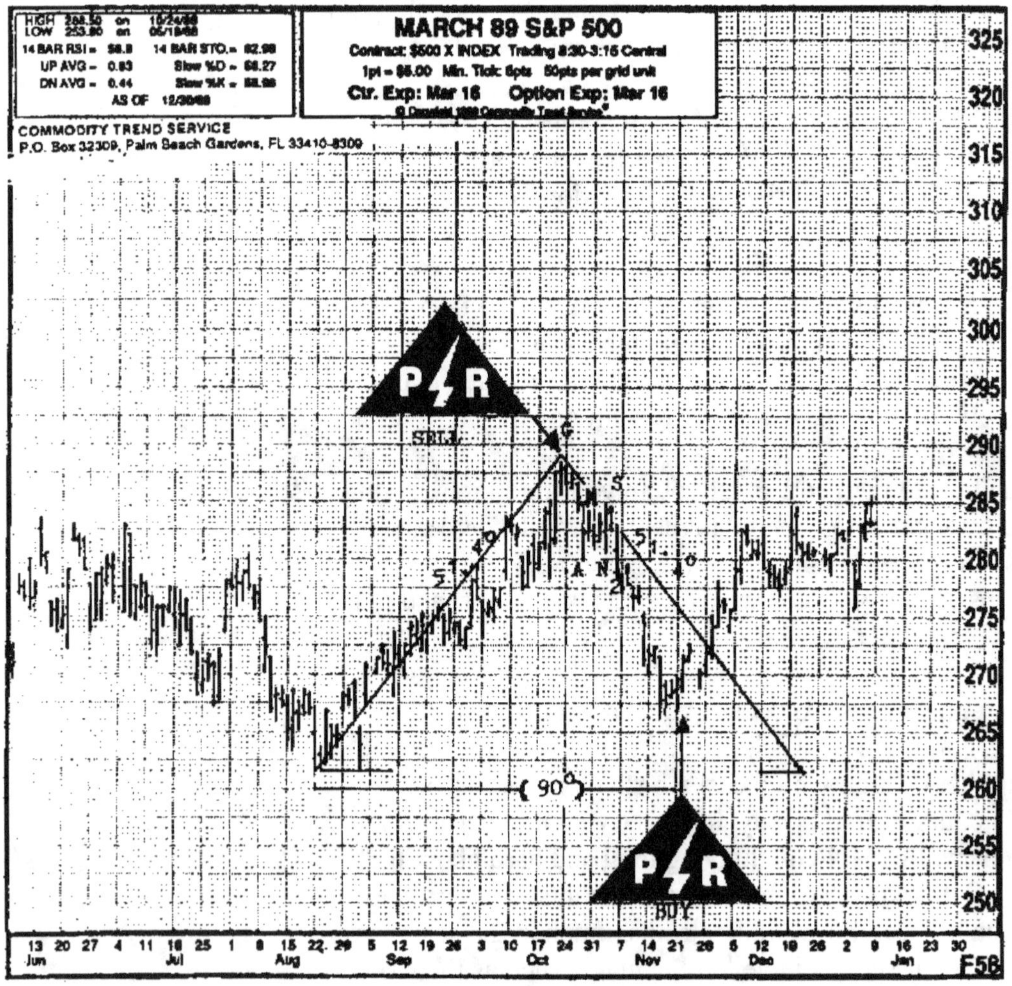

On page 55 in W.D. Gann's book. How to Profit From Commodities, Gann states, you will always make the most profit by following the main trend and playing the long swing. You can never make much money jumping in and out of the market trying to scalp it. If you will put in time and study to determine the main trend, and then follow it the length of time that it should run and not get Out until you get a definite indication of change in trend, you will make big profits. It is much better to make three or four trades each year and make large profits than it is to try to make 100 to 200 trades a year and be wrong half the time, and finally wind up with a net loss. Yet there are times when it will pay to stay out of the market and wait for a definite indication and a real opportunity, which is sure to come if you wait.

After 14 years of research and reflection, I've come to realize the profound wisdom of W.D. Gann's statement, that in order to make the greatest profit one must trade with the long-term trend.

A major error is to focus on one or two favorite indicators, thus losing sight of the overall big picture.

In previous articles of the Gann & Elliott Wave, I have revealed some of the valuable trading tools and techniques to follow W.D. Gann's philosophy of how to make big profits.

In order to define the long-term trend, one must focus on, and look at the complete picture. To properly define the long-term trend, all of W.D. Gann's most valuable trading tools and techniques must be used and integrated into proper market analysis. This involves extensively following many indicators, as the weight of the evidence will determine when and how to enter a long term position trade and where to place stops for proper risk management.

A tremendous aid for following and analyzing Gann's most valuable trading tools and techniques on several different stock, option and futures markets comes through the use of computer technology. My long-term goal to computerize W.D. Gann's most valuable trading tools and techniques is complete.

Pat Reda, my long time associate, has provided the computer technology link for the past four years to finally achieve this goal. Pat has researched Gann and Elliott for the past seven years in the stock, options and futures markets, and is an electrical engineer with an extensive background in computer architecture and software design. He has designed software around the Gann Wheel and the Square of Nine chart in order to facilitate mathematical harmony of market movements in time and price.

Together we have developed an ultimate trading system which generates a disciplined set of rules to obtain major buy and sell signals with short-term risk parameters in any stock, options or futures market.

Past articles in the Gann & Elliott Wave magazine have provided the forum to release some of W.D. Gann's most valuable tools and techniques in order to assist others to help themselves and make themselves independent, successful traders. In conclusion, I want to make you aware of Pythagoras Aphorism Number four, which states assist a man in raising or lifting his burden; but do not assist him in laying it down. Once one learns the disciplines and sets of rules to follow W.D. Gann's most valuable trading tools and techniques, then and only then will it be your time to make the greatest profits by following the main trend and playing the long swing!

Reference to the chart of the S&P500 clearly points out some of the most valuable trading tools and techniques used by W.D. Gann.

The Gann Wheel on May 1989 Coffee reprint (1.5)

By Jim Purucker and Pat Reda

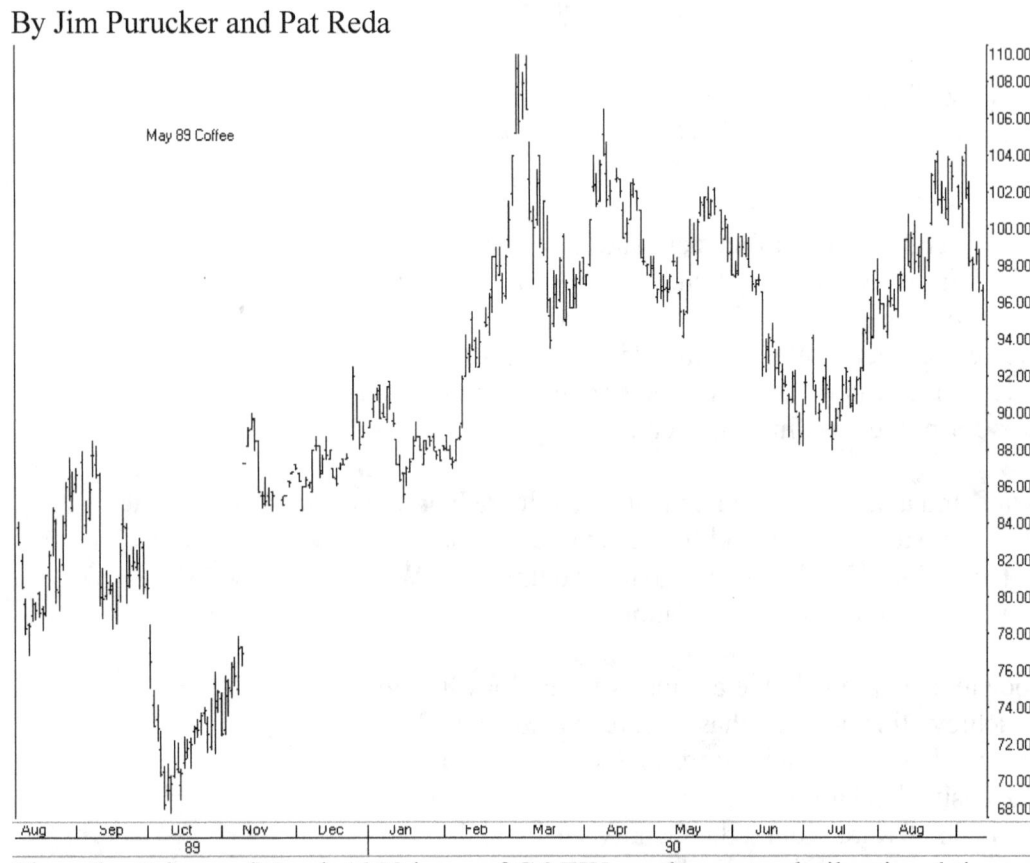

Since the February/March 1989 issue of G&EW another natural vibrational time-trend change cause and effect timing point occurred the week beginning February 20, 1989.

Specifically, a trade was presented from this natural timing point on the May 1989 coffee from the long side.

In chapter three of W.D. Gann's book, "How to Make Profits in Commodities," Gann states, "Time is the most important factor of all and not until sufficient time has expired does any big move start up or down. Time must be allowed for accumulation or distribution before the trend can change."

Once you are aware of when these natural timing points occur, the next step is to watch for the G-A-N-N2 Buy/Sell price pattern to form. This pattern allows plenty of time (3-4 weeks) to visually see accumulation or distribution to take place.

The May 1989 coffee trade starts from the zero degree natural cause and effect week of February 20, 1989, marked (G) on the chart. The high price of January 3,

1989, at 159.20 to the low price on February 21, 1989 at 122.90 was 3 squares of 90° on the Gann Wheel.

Next, follow Gann's rule #25, page 44 in "How to Make Profits in Commodities," "Don't guess when the market is at bottom. Let the market prove it is at bottom." From the low in May 1989 coffee at 122.90 a rally occurs into the week of March 13, 1989, making a high in price on March 17, 1989 at 135.24. This was one square of price 90 degrees from the 122.90 low and 180 degrees opposition from the 159.20 high of January 3, 1989 on the Gann Wheel, marked (A) on the chart. Three market days later, on March 22, 1989, as the accumulation pattern continues to build, the low or (N) marked on the chart, is put in place. The following day the (N2) of the price pattern is formed. From this point, more time is needed for the price to drop below the (N) low to trigger our actual buy recommendation on the P/R Futures Hotline broadcast, to buy one contract of May '89 Coffee @126.15 on 3-28-89. Initial protective stop 124.15. On the Sunday, April 2nd P/R Futures Hotline broadcast, the protective stop was raised to 125.45.

On the Tuesday, April 4th, P/R Futures Hotline broadcast, the protective stop was raised to our break-even entry point of 126.15. On the Thursday, April 6th P/R Futures Hotline broadcast, the stop remained at 126.15. On the Sunday, April 9th P/R Futures Hotline broadcast, the protective stop was raised to 128.15. On the Tuesday, April 11th P/R Futures Hotline broadcast, we recommended an additional long contract of May '89 Coffee @ 1st Order Vibrational Price Support of 131.95 M.IT. The protective stop was raised on the entire position to 130.15. On Wednesday, April 12th, we bought @ 131.95. On the Thursday, April 13th P/R Futures Hotline broadcast, we recommended to hold the 2 long May '89 Coffee contracts with a protective stop @ 130. 15. On the Sunday, April 16th, P/R Futures Hotline broadcast we recommended to buy a third May '89 Coffee contract at 2nd Order Vibrational Price Line Support @ 134.30. The protective stop was raised on the entire position to 131.15, which was just below the final Major 1st Order Vibrational Price Line Support of 132.85. This final Vibrational-Price Line Support @ 132.85 must hold in order to maintain the up trend in May '89 Coffee. A price breakdown below this level would reverse the psychology of the Coffee market, thus turning the trend decisively lower below the 2nd Order Vibrational Price Line Support of 134.30. The last line of major support was 90° lower at the 1st Order Vibrational Price Line of 132.85, as mentioned previously. 1 32.85 was the opening price and the exact low of the day where we bought the third May '89 Coffee contract @ 132.85. Protective stop is 131.15 on the entire position. On Monday, April 17th, this final Major 1st Order Vibrational Price Line of 132.85 held and launched a major rally to close that day @138.85. Once again, the market has proven itself by picking up the energy for launch at the Major Vibrational Price Line Support on the Gann Wheel, confirming to all P/R Futures Hotline Subscribers, the major trend remained very bullish.

On the Tuesday, April 18th P/R Futures Hotline broadcast, we recommended to sell 2 contracts of May '89 Coffee @141.90 M.I.T., which was the Vibrational Price Line objective on the Gann Wheel, as well as a 50% retracement at the center of gravity from the contract high on 1-3-89 @ 159.20 and the 3-21-89 Low @ 122.90.

On Thursday, April 20th, we sold 2 contracts on May '89 Coffee @141.90. On the Thursday, April 20th P/R Futures Hotline broadcast we recommended selling the remaining contract on the open Friday, due to 1st notice day on the May '89 Coffee.

On Friday, April 21st, we sold the remaining contract @ 139.10. The closed profit on the three long May'89 positions was $11,981.25 in 19 market days.

THE GANN WHEEL, OCTAGON CHART, PYTHAGOREAN CUBE, SQUARE OF 9

By Daniel T. Ferrera

The Square of 9 is basically a spiral of numbers starting with the number one in the center (or apex of the Great Pyramid) with the number 2 immediately to the left. See the Square of 9 Chart on page 18 of this magazine. The rest of the numbers spiral around the center in a clockwise fashion to the number 9, which completes the first cycle of numbers around the center. 10 through 25 completes the 2nd cycle, 26 through 49 completes the 3rd, etc. This particular arrangement of numbers creates a very unique square root relationship with other numbers on the chart. Michael S. Jenkins illustrates some interesting square root trading techniques utilizing the square of 9 in his book Chart Reading for Professional Traders, available from Traders World. Basically, if you want to move around the coordinates on the Gann Wheel you take the number your are interested in (such as the all time High or Low price) take the square root of the number, then add or subtract 2 from the root and re square the result. Example: Lets say that we are interested in the price 664 (which is in the vertical column straight up from the center). The square root is $25.768 + 2 = 27.768^2 = 771$ which is the number directly above 664 or one full 360 degree cycle out from the center. If we subtracted 2 from the root and re-squared the number ($25.768-2 = 23.768^2 = 564$) we would get 564, which is directly below 664 or one full 360 degree cycle in towards center. Incorporating the Gann Emblem with this technique, allows us to calculate coordinates that are conjunct ($360 = +/-2$ from the root), opposition ($180 = +/-1$ from root #), trine ($120 = +/- .666$) ($240 = +/- 1.333$), square ($90 = +/- .5$) ($270 = +/- 1.5$) and sextile * ($60 = +/- .333$) ($300 = +/- 1.666$). This technique is extremely useful for finding coordinate squares on the Gann Wheel that are making hard aspects to a previous position on the wheel. Also, Gann believed that the numbers that connected the square base of the pyramid (the 4 corners of the square, I.E. Corner #'s) to the "gravity center" and also the numbers that ran straight vertical and horizontal from the "gravity center" in the form of a cross (cardinal numbers) were very important in balancing "Price & Time" on the wheel. He was basically looking for astronomical longitudes to balance with price on these key angles. Pythagoras said "Units in a circle or in a square are related to each other in terms of Price & Time at specific points." Gann often quoted the Bible, Emerson, Pythagoras and Faraday to name a few. Basically, he was pointing the reader of his works to clues that would allow his student to unlock the code of his writing style.

Around the out perimeter of the square of 9 is a circle with months and days. The circular calendar starts on the right hand side of the wheel on the same horizontal line as the center block. The data is March 21st and refers to the start of the "natural year" in the season of Spring with the Sun in Aries (the ram). "Lamb of

God you take away the sins of the world" (Spring takes away the sins of Winter). The dates move around the circle counter clockwise completing the calendar. This relationship allow the user to quickly identify dates that are Conjunct, Opposite, Square, Trine, or sextile to a post turning date relative to the Sun/Earth relationship.

In Gann's Master Course for Stocks he said "Within the circle forms the square, there is an inner circle and an inner square, as well as an outer square and an outer circle which prove the Fourth Dimension in working out price movements." So far, we have covered the inner circle (The Earth's Orbit around the Sun) and the inner square (Historic high & low coordinates on the square itself). The outer circle is the Zodiac starting at the left side of the square opposite March 21st on the calendar date September 23rd. This is where the Earth is in the zodiac when the Sun in Aries. Moving from this point clockwise in 30 degree sections of the circle will place the zodiac symbols around the wheel. This completes the outer circle and allows the analyst to examine planetary relationships to price coordinates on the Square of 9, which is now, an outer square. The inner square moves counter clockwise, the outer square clockwise relative to the circle (see attached square of 9). In this way, we can convert planetary positions to prices relating to degrees of a circle (Zodiac longitude) and also to coordinates on the square of 9. We can also examine hard aspects to both zodiac longitude and Square of 9 coordinates. Furthermore, we can also use a first trade chart (Natal Chart), i.e. horoscope (another inner circle) to locate sensitive longitude positions that are being aspected by planets from the other circle making them "Live Angles"! Is there any end to this multidimensional tool? Gann hinted about this natal horoscope technique in his Master Course for Stocks by saying "The dates when companies are incorporated and the dates when stocks are first traded in on the New York Exchange or the other exchanges causes them to make tops and bottoms at slightly different dates then these dates for seasonal changes". Gann also illustrated this technique in his astro letter, which is well worth reading. I believe that this is what Gann meant when he discussed "Natural Law".
Gann said "Through the law of vibration every stock and commodity in the market place moves in its own distinctive sphere of activities," (natal horoscope?) "As to intensity, volume and direction. All the essential qualities of its evolution are characterized in its own rate of vibration. Stocks and commodities, like atoms, are really centers of energies, therefore they are controlled mathematically. They create their own field of action and power, to attract and repel, and which explains why certain stocks and commodities at times lead the market and turn dead at other times. Thus, to speculate scientifically it is absolutely necessary to follow Natural Law. Vibration is fundamental; nothing is exempt from its law. It is universal, therefore applicable to every class of phenomena on the globe. Thus, I affirm every class of phenomena, whether in nature or in the market, must be subject to the universal laws by causation, harmony and vibration." Gann also said "My calculations are based on supply and demand and are purely scientific, mathematical calculations. Many years ago I discovered a time factor which

enables me to tell when accumulation or distribution is taking place and when stocks reach approximate tops or bottoms." Gann called his newsletter service the Supply & Demand Letter. Compare this last quote from Gann with a rise with a quote from Louise McWhirter's 1938 book McWhirter's Theory of Stock Market Forecasting: "The rise and fall of price is governed by the law of Supply and Demand. Which is in turn governed by the law in the universe, hitherto unknown or ignored, known as the law of Action and Reaction. Periods of business prosperity and depression are not man made nor the result of chance; they come at regular intervals, the same as the seasons, and the same astronomical laws which govern nature, govern man and all man's activities. When this fact is recognized, man will work in harmony with the force of nature and not blindly against them."

Nobody knows for certain how Gann used this Master Calculator, but if you will study this material and apply the techniques presented in this article. I think you will agree that this is how Gann probably using this tool which proves the "4th" dimension in working out time and price movements".

One of Gann's most amazing calculations came during the summer of 1909 when he predicted that the September contract of wheat would sell at $120. This meant that it must hit this price before the end of September before contract expiration. At 12 o'clock Chicago time, on September 30th (the very last trading date for the Sept. wheat) was selling below $1.08. It looked as through Gann would be wrong! Gann said" If it does not touch $1.20 by the close of the market it will prove there is something wrong with my whole method of calculation. I do not care what the price is now it must go there." It is now common history that September wheat sold at $1.20 and no higher in the very last hour of trading and closed at this figure surprising the whole country. If you cast a horoscope for September 30th 1909, you will find that Mars was in opposition to Jupiter, also look at the Sun/Earth relationship to price and natal aspects to price. If you place these planets on the outer zodiac circle on the Gann Wheel, you will see that Jupiter & Mars longitude where making aspects to the price of $1.20 on the Square of 9. That natal planets are on the outer wheel and the planetary positions for 9/30/09 are on the inner wheel.

Gann's Secret Pythagorean Cube

By Don Hall

Many manuscripts and seminars have been presented regarding trading stocks, bonds, and commodities. Indeed, trading has a very unique and ancient history, dating back to the earliest recordings of any type of commerce.

No one will expound for long on the simplicity of the challenge; and again, no one denies that it is a mammoth challenge. The percentage of failures versus the percentages of triumphs will attest to this. It has been said that more people fail at this profession than most commercial businesses. It is also a known fact that the percentage ratio of wins to losses is definitely on the side of the losses.
Realizing this, some 40 years ago we set goals that we felt needed to be addressed (and indeed, answered) by any so-called trading system. From our earliest studies we defined our system needs to do at least the following:

1. Establish trend
2. Have mathematical and ongoing stop placement
3. Have realistic and accurate objectives in any move
4. Know mathematically when a move has started and when it is culminated
5. Know at all times -- in any trade -- where we are in our planned objective
6. Provide peace of mind to the trader to avert being ill with anxiety
  overnight or even during the day.

To us this meant the graphic source of considerable information should be easily digested and interpreted.

TO US THIS SUGGESTED A SQUARE WITHIN THE PARAMETERS OF OUR CURRENT TRADING! We had not seen such a drawing available to us. This led our studies toward Gann, Brenner, Bayer and Company.
 When my father passed away in 1961 I recall that I was charting extensively -- and trading some.

I went through all of the stages from Point and Figure to Moving Averages, collected all the books on everyone's mailing list, it seemed, and then settled upon following the studies of a man who has shown us to be one of the most successful commodity traders of all time, Mr. W.D. Gann. This decision was supported by a fortunate event wherein I received the opportunity to retrace his path into Egypt and along the Nile.

History shows us that Mr. Gann made three trips abroad that were of significance to his studies: to England, to India and to Egypt.

He had one of the best history and data sources of the day, and much of this was acquired in English libraries and museums. We have studied much of this. Second, he was known to be very astute in mathematical circles. Much of this credit has been attributed to his trips to India and places where, we are told, he studied a very unique and effective math system. This system has been compared to our earliest studies of what we now call "modern math." At any rate, he learned to use floating decimal procedures and he was very proficient in the use of numbers.

The third important trip abroad seemed to culminate, and indeed concentrate, in Egypt. Not as much seems to be known of these Egyptian studies. Our quest became to learn the objective of this particular phase of his studies. We believe that we have accomplished this. Certainly he rated along with the greats: Livermore, Brenner, Bayer, Barouch and others.

He was especially known for his commodity trading which was considered tougher than stocks because of the leverage.

From the early '60's when I began to study somewhat in earnest, and following at least to the mid-seventies, I attended many seminars, but I especially attempted to attend all seminars available on Gann.

Alas, however! I never found the secret as shown by his verified results.
It was only after attending most of the Gann seminars, administered by people all of whom were claiming to have his secret, that I came to the conclusion that there was a question as to whether the teachers were actually duplicating his record. Indeed, they were usually not even in fair range of his results.

It was then that I began dissecting his seminars and assimilating certain segments of different seminars. I came to some conclusions, not the least of which was, in my opinion:

THAT HE WASN'T ALWAYS TEACHING THAT WHICH HE WAS ACTUALLY TRADING.

I can stand corrected, but the next ten years proved to me the validity of my convictions. Mr. Gann indicated that he would not reveal the true secret of the math involved. However, he also indicated that if one were to spend the time which he had (25 years) and covered the material at least three times, that it could be revealed to a serious student.

I have qualified for the years, plus some -- sometimes to the exhaustion of my family, I'm sure.

I SUBMIT TO YOU THAT THE PYRAPOINT SYSTEM IS THE PRINCIPLE THAT HE USED. We can prove it, I feel. But if you will accept our point, in our book we intend to spend our time with "hands-on" proof so that we can learn the true and full potential of the system. This is why we go to a seminar and why we study the manual.

Incidentally, we should have no copyright infringements because, to our knowledge and research, Mr. Gann never taught this in any of his seminars, even to his associate, who I had the privilege to personally know for some seven years, Mr. Renato Alghini. "Reno" was with Gann for six years, actually sharing close trading desks. Reno confirmed the extremely private personality of his friend. This is shown in most of Gann's writings and seminars.

Reno passed away a few years ago. However, during the author's years of acquaintance with him, he shared a few facts that made the direction of our efforts truly appear validated. One of the confirmation factors seemed especially worthwhile in the revelation that Gann carried a small paper in hand when in the "pit" for his most successfully recorded trades. This paper, Reno related, was a miniature Pythagorean Cube. One more reason to believe that we had to unravel this mystic marvel -- and that we were, indeed, on the right track for trading understanding.

Mr. Gann died in 1956.

It is significant to note that a favorite statement of Gann serves us well when we state that we believe that EVERY TOP AND EVERY BOTTOM in the markets have a CALCULABLE counterpart -- a formula for projections and targets for both PRICE and for TIME. His quotes included that of the noted mathematician Faraday. Mr. Gann said, "If we wish to avert failure in speculation, we must deal with causes. Everything in existence is based on exact proportion and perfect relationship. There is no chance in nature, because mathematical principles of the highest order lie at the foundation of all things." Faraday said: "There is nothing in the Universe but mathematical points of force."

THIS IS THE TRUE BASIS OF THE PYRAPOINT SYSTEM OF TRADING. Although we give full credit to Gann, Wycoff, Brenner, Jenson, Bayer and other contemporaries of earlier times for their contributions to mathematical approaches to the markets, we must tell you that this is likely not what was being sold in $5000 seminars. We sincerely believe that PYRAPOINT is what they so successfully traded.

Gann and Company reportedly used many "squares" -- the more important often included such numbers as 3, 4, 12, 15, 24, 45, 72, 90, 144, 180 and 360, we are told. Gann has been quoted as saying that one must compute TIME, based upon PRICE.

THIS WE DO.

Gann also is reported to have indicated that PRICE must be seen or projected upon a circle -- then he said that the circle had to be squared to obtain the TIME for trend changes in the market.
THIS WE ALSO DO.

Although we have enlisted the assistance of a programmer to place PYRAPOINT on the TradeStation format, it is easy to hand-draw and hand-calculate when all data is in place.

A number of variations of the Pythagorean Cube are available. We have used the format as used by Forrest Wilke of Lincoln, Nebraska, in his version of the "Square of Nine Gann Wheel."

Relative to the charting technique, we acknowledge two specific factors that will assist your learning process: (1) Since our approach to charting is presented as Universal, it is obvious that more than one lesson should show on a chart. It should be ongoing. Thus we can show repetitive charts with an additional lesson blending into the sister chart. (2) Since you will be examining specific entry/exit and other finite points of interest, you may find that an "exploded view" may, at times, better serve you to clarify the total picture so that you can place it into the larger picture -- a larger degree, if you will.

Although no emphasis is placed upon the supporting momentum charts that we use from time to time, we do sometimes apply inputs that we consider to be compatible to PYRAPOINT. This should not materially change your understanding or your learning of the study.

The derivative of the PYRAPOINT system is the result of our experience of some 35 years, wherein we have tried all of the systems which are likely in your portfolio as well, discarding and trying again, until finally coming to the conclusion that we would need to clear out the massive amounts of underbrush (and there are piles of it) -- and to see if core data didn't have some common thread. It is our opinion that we have, indeed, found the Universal Thread. Heard that one before? Read it in an article (or a hundred or so) perhaps?
BUT READ ON -- WE PROMISE YOU MORE POTENTIAL THAN YOU ARE USED TO RECEIVING.

First, let us examine some of the background and origins of our compiled data that essentially makes up a majority of our CORE DATA.

Part is taken from the lessons that I feel that W.D. Gann learned while in Egypt, and specifically in the study of the Great Pyramid, and its dimensions. Part is the

Universal Golden Ratio, but used in a CALCULATED manner to make up the Gann-Type Squares. It is the study of this that brings us to core data that we will use. The heart of the whole system depends upon a calculation and the interpretation of the Gann "Square of Nine." This likely goes back to Brenner, Bayer, Gann, and eventually back to the real core in the Pythagorean Cube (as well as the early Egyptian Calendar, we are told).

To answer as to the history of the PYRAPOINT Trading System, we need to start with the core data and the core authors. To do this, we begin with Pythagoras who lived, as did Socrates, a few hundred years +/-, A.D.

Some historians tell us that Pythagoras, like Socrates, was guilty of teaching the common man in early Greece. We say "guilty" because Socrates got the Hemlock juice for teaching outside of the Priesthood. Since this was the primary manner of control for the hierarchy, they naturally frowned upon this type of teaching. Thus it was, we are told, that Pythagoras took exile to Egypt where he stayed 22 years -- the time it took to complete the Priesthood.

Is it any wonder that the "father of our mathematics" (especially the geometric math) was able to bring back to Greece all that he learned in the "cradle of mathematical civilization" of that day? It included such things as that which we base our system upon even today. Mr. Gann learned this from his trip to Egypt, in our opinion, because at the top of the learning list were our vital and basic tools -- the square, the circle and the Hypotenuse Rule. These: Phi, Pi, Square Root, and squaring of a number are addressed later for your application in your understanding of the PYRAPOINT Trading System.

This "revelation" given by Pythagoras in the first few centuries A.D. is still Universally accepted, and it is evident from the smallest snail, through the life and body of man and plant, through the Milky Way. This is an ever onward, ever outward process, and is indeed in the markets as well. The learning of this process is at the core of our learning system.

One last passing observation: the tools to which we referred as primary in the marketplace, and indeed in our PYRAPOINT System of Trading, are found in the Great Pyramid of Giza which was built 2500 years before Pythagoras. Doesn't it make one wonder what took place in that 2500 years since all of the above-mentioned tools are evident in the Pyramids and the tombs? It is our conclusion that Gann had to realize this from his personal trips to Egypt, as the author personally did when in Cairo and associated areas that he had the privilege to study, in the area all along the Nile River. This included the quarries where some granite was perfectly formed to Phi proportions, evident in the manner of relationship of the height to base, and which are reported to weigh literally tons. We have avoided inclusion of many of the very fascinating theories advanced by the Egyptians themselves relative to the Great Pyramid. In passing, let us say that we have relayed to you only the things which relate to the markets, and which we have had the privilege of observations and determination.

Worthy of mention are a couple of theories advanced by a college-educated contact (the author's guide during his stay in Egypt) especially as related to the Great Pyramid:

(1) The limestone-clad granite structure covering 13 acres and extending more than 450' in height is credited with carrying very exacting dimensions. An early Egyptian mathematical index, which they used, accurately projects the distance to the sun (from its height), the mass of the earth (from its mass), and the circumference of the earth at its largest mile (from its perimeter).

(2) Mummification seems a characteristic of the Pyramid -- not found outside. Without question, we are studying results of universally prime information -- and we can show you that it is primary (and indeed the key) to the markets.
Our question has been how should this learning be best conducted in the manual? Our answer to you: in the simplest, most straightforward manner that we can, to get you to be able to USE the System. This will be a hands-on trading system/study -- you must be able to use the information, even if you have to accept some information for later proof. Our plan is to present to you the schedule of information which you need for this learning process. We will not dwell on the process so that we might spend productive time in the "hands-on" role with actual charts (complete with commentary and instructions.) We believe that this is where the true worth of any system is weighed. It is our opinion that it must be used effectively, and in first person, for one to get a full appreciation of just how real and how consistent potential returns can be with this system.
The charts will truly act as 1000 words. It is our intent to call your attention to basic "setups" in many different topics of various trading subjects and of various time frames as well. This will assist you in learning the UNIVERSALITY as well as FLEXIBILITY of PYRAPOINT.

To use the PYRAPOINT technique, please realize that we are not asking that you discard any of your learned good trading rules. We do ask that, since we are operating on a totally calculated line and square, that you follow what we have learned to be a very highly accurate set of simple rules. The nice part of this technique is that it can overlay any theory or system that may presently be of interest or in use by you. Even if you choose not to use PYRAPOINT as your primary theorem, please look at the rules and squares for confirmation. WE ARE BETTING THAT YOU WILL CHANGE YOUR PRIMARY UNIT!

The rules which we use are self-evident on your chart of the square for the price parameter in which your commodity or stock is trading. We operate upon the theory that if we can successfully trade the square representing the parameter currently trading then, in all probability, we will have success in the next square as well. Thus, the rules that we submit for this square will be universally acceptable for any commodity or stock that you will be trading. The only preface which we caution is to fit the TIME unit and the PRICE unit into scales that are "common sense" to the parameters of price and volatility. In other words, use a square size that will reflect the manner in which the unit is trading. One way of confirming this "common sense" is to realize that it would take a considerably smaller square to reflect the action of an hourly chart of a low-volatility commodity or stock than it would take for a daily or even a weekly, especially in high-volatility status. Again, this should not be a primary worry for you. PYRAPOINT and your own judgment will suffice as soon as you become acquainted. Actually, you can see the picture with very little experience. The worst scenario that you might have is working with a square that is within a square. It is all repetitive, "ever onward, ever outward." You are simply the recorder of a very Universal and Wonderful Law. As soon as you have the ability to build a square from data provided to you, then you are ready to find out what all of these lines really represent. All of this is governed by six simple and totally defined rules.

Given the nature and complexity of trading, we need to KNOW WHERE WE ARE AT A GIVEN TIME, WHAT WE SHOULD EXPECT AS A MODE FOR EACH PRICE LEVEL, AND WHAT TO DO WHEN IT CHANGES -- and it will change!! Just be ready!!

Technical trading has been referenced to trend lines or trading lines, which make up a parameter for rules of trading. PYRAPOINT is no different in that particular regard. Therefore, we have set upon a path or plan to define these lines, establish the parameters, define the parameters, and then to provide the reasoning behind the rules which make up PYRAPOINT's system -- just as other systems which you have studied. What is different in the study is the CALCULATION and its methodology, and the rules for application within each of the parameters of each square.

These are some of the studies/theorems which Pythagorous brought back to Greece and which are covered to make PYRAPOINT valid:

(1) Tools of the PYRAPOINT System are found in The Great Pyramid -- as are tools of the circle. They include:
a. Pi
b. Phi
c. Square Root
d. Square of Number
e. Hypotenuse Rule

(2) Pythagorean Cube is the core of the PYRAPOINT System of Trading.

(3) PYRAPOINT unveils mysteries of the Pythagorean Cube -- the Square of Nine -- Egyptian Calendar.

(4) PYRAPOINT interprets moves of the markets as reflected on the "P.C."

(5) PYRAPOINT identifies calculated squares for every parameter of price.

(6) PYRAPOINT lets you graphically know where to enter (whether buying or selling) and gives the highway to travel to maintain the position profitably.

(7) PYRAPOINT tells you when to expect a trend change, gives you the objective both long and short until the time frame and beyond.

(8) PYRAPOINT gives you the exact action per your position in the calculated square at any, and at all times.

(9) The Trading System works in all denominations of time frames, allowing you to confirm as well as plan. PYRAPOINT also allows all time frames to be correlated into reasonable and profitable squares -- even with small/large price ranges or small/large time frames.

(10) PYRAPOINT operates on the mathematical information that every top and every bottom has a mathematical counterpart -- and herein lies the opportunity to project the action of the market -- and to profit there from (11) The System unlocks the relationship of PRICE and TIME and squares them on a 360 degree circle for each move.

At this juncture, it would seem that the all-important Pythagorean Cube (the "P.C.") should be further described. You will note that a sample of the tool is provided. It is shown as a number series, beginning with number 1 in the center, and progressing ever-onward and ever-outward in a spiral of spaces in sequence. It also has the characteristic that it is divided evenly in fourths, eighths, sixteenths, etc., as the numbers progress in the circle.

In the "P.C.'s" pure state, before any added divisions, it is reported to be a calendar as used by early Egyptians. We personally find this to be a very interesting synopsis since it, too, would date back far earlier than the celebrated works of Pythagoras.

One of the things we do know about the Egyptians' early use of the "P.C." is that it was used in their mathematical teachings and usage. IT IS AN UNERRING CALCULATOR IN THE WORK TO WHICH WE APPLY IT.

The "P.C." was further refined by scholars such as W.D. Gann (and likely Brenner, Bayer and others) for use in calculating trading strategies. Since Gann, for instance, made his famous studies and seminars around the establishment of PRICE and TIME as projected on a circle, it follows that this tool would lend itself to circular measurement and, indeed, fractions thereof. Gann called this

"P.C." a MASTER CALCULATOR for his famous work.
To use the calculator to its fullest support level in their calculations, scholars such as Gann have divided the circle as applied by the "P.C." into divisions of the 360° circle which it depicts. They have also given TIME as well as PRICE divisions or sections as shown in this calculator.

It is the author's opinion that our ability to unravel these mysteries as Mr. Gann did will give a trader the best edge at trading which is available today -- perhaps the best known to man!

Bibliography:

1. The W. D. Gann Commodity Trading Course by W.D. Gann, Lambert-Gann Publishing Co., Inc

2. How to Make Profits in Commodities, by W.D. Gann, Lambert-Gann Publishing Co. Inc.

2. Gann Masters Trading Course, Halliker's, Inc.

3. Master Table Charts for Time & Price Projection, Halliker's, Inc.

4. Top Secret Trading Techniques, Halliker's, Inc.

5. The Gann & Elliott Wave Magazine, Halliker's, Inc.

6. Traders World Magazine, Halliker's, Inc.

7. Pyrapoint, by Don Hall

Thanks to Nikki Jones for giving us permission to use pictures of the hand-drawn charts from the original W.D. Gann Commodity Course. You can purchase the original Gann Course and many of his books from the Lambert Gann Publishing Company at www.wdgann.com

Thanks to all the Gann traders who gave us information on how they trade the Gann methodology regarding the square, the circle, the hexagon chart, etc.

The charts in this book are produced from the excellent data chart package from Commodity Systems, Inc., Unfair Advantage. www.csidate.com

The Gann Masters Course is available from us on our website at www.tradersworld.com

The templates in this book were produced from the Microsoft Excel spreadsheet program.

Most the Excel charts in this book are available in template form from the CD ROM, which is also attached to this book. Remember you can expand the charts in this book by using the simple techniques of the Excel software program.

www.ingramcontent.com/pod-product-compliance
Lightning Source LLC
Chambersburg PA
CBHW081828170526
45167CB00007B/2748